The Metaphix

THE METAPHIX

BY CATHY COLBURN

WITH

E. Alexander Riegelmann

A Lionhead Press Publication

Printed in the United States of America

ISBN-13: 978-0-9892285-3-4

First Edition

For My Teachers:

Janice Lindgren - You helped me realize that I was lost and to start the quest to find myself.

Julie Hutlsar - You reconnected me with my spirit, and taught me how to trust my intuition.

Jacki Beem - You helped me go beyond my wildest dreams and then to keep going.

vi

Contents

Foreword

By Julie Hutslar

Everyone has a gift. Most people either don't realize it's unique or they don't know they have it. They just came packaged with it. These are our personal gifts.

Cathy Colburn's is the way she thinks and the way she communicates these unusual ways of seeing things. She has the uncanny ability to understand and relate to both artists and scientists, right-and-left-brain thinkers. In my experience, this is quite unique. She also speaks metaphor, which is usually only found in poets and artists, not scientists. Yet she always seems to find an amazingly accurate metaphor for whoever she is speaking with and is able to connect and enlighten.

Somehow she can turn on a light bulb in a confused mind. She seems to reach in and see where the disconnect is and untangle the knots or turn on the light. In the years I have been working with people, helping them remove limiting beliefs about themselves, I have very few people I trade with, mostly because I realize that the beliefs I can't reach are sneaky, hidden in remote recesses of my non-conscious mind. It requires a different sort of thinking, not direct and logical, neither phantasmagorical or flighty, but something sneaky, I guess.

Yes, you guessed it, Cathy can do it. She has this rare ability to appear soft and unsuspecting, you let down your inner defenses and then she seems to tickle the bugger out, somehow. I really don't know, it is simply a unique gift she has, it appears effortless on her part. She can not only find it, but she can use the exact words and analogies to make it all seem so logical or evident that releasing it feels super easy. She can also communicate with people on the autism spectrum, those who have reading disorders or difficulties in learning and shed light, understanding and realization! Sometimes she is a catalyst, unbeknownst to her, saying the thing that pushes someone over. Either they find themselves on the other side of a barrier that was limiting their lives, or they point the blame finger at her. That's the other side of this gift. She just casually drops water into the beaker as she walks by. What happens depends on what was in the beaker.

So thinking that Cathy wrote a book coming from that unusual mind of hers, collating all the tools she has picked up, then translated them into her unique language, I would read it. Chances are, she is speaking your language. Chances are, you will learn something, probably without even knowing you are growing or changing.

Introduction

The first time I heard about personal growth, I knew that it would never be something I would want to do. I knew it was good for some, but I knew I would never need it, because I was fine; I had a good childhood, and had good relationships with the people in my life. What I didn't know was a lot. I didn't know what my future would be. And I didn't know how I would come to wish I started the second I first heard about it.

The way I see it now, is that it gave me the tools before I needed to rely on them. The first Metaphor I will use is... It's like going to the hardware store before you start the project instead of during. Personal growth isn't only to help heal from older wounds, it is also to help you through difficult times that may come, or to help others through those times.

Personally my wounds seemed subtle and almost peaceful, yet I have now learned how much they have affected my current daily life. Sometimes the wounds were so subtle that I could only use a metaphor to understand it. And even heal it. I find using metaphor alone helps me face things that may seem too much to face.

I have also personally found that the tools I use to manage stressful situations have improved my health. I carry less tension physically, and my mind races much less on imagined fears. That is not to claim that I am immune to stress and difficult times, or health concerns. I believe that they reduce the amount of time I spend in stress and difficulty therefore reducing the amount of time that my body is under more stress. The tools help me face discomfort promptly, communicate more gracefully, and hold a bigger picture of each situation.

What I hope to do with this book is to show you some tools and how to use them. If you are inspired to pursue any topic deeper, I invite you to check into the sources that I learned from myself. There is a list of books that have helped me that go a bit deeper.

My own story is a compiling list of stresses that kept accruing. They were spread out over time, so I felt that I was managing. But with each event, the stress kept accumulating. Like drips in a bucket. Eventually the bucket filled up and I felt overburdened and didn't know why. Somehow

I found myself at a workshop that taught me how to release some burdens, how to find a safe place inside myself, and how to communicate to others in a new way. I followed that workshop with another and another and another. From a variety of places that offered them. I attended almost twelve a year for a few years. And then I only slowed the pace. I continue to attend and learn, but those first years resulted in a change in my life perspective.

My goal is to share bits of each of the workshops that I attended over the years. Some tools might not be a fit for you, and others you might use daily. My hope is to expose you to a new way to be. A way that is more peaceful and calm.

Each time of my life that had difficulty, I wondered what I would do to help me. What would I say to myself if I could go back to those moments? Each time I would encourage myself to relax in spite of the circumstances. They also led me to be more relaxed during difficult times not just personally but also on a society level. These tools help me do this.

And now, I hope you do this also.

PART I: BELIEF

1. Evolution

WHY EVOLVE?

I watched a show once in which a woman purchased her mother's house. The mother warned her about a tree growing in the backyard—she said it needed to be trimmed. The daughter considered it a low priority and procrastinated. Until one morning, when a branch of the tree came crashing through the kitchen window.

The mother said, "I told you it needed to be trimmed," and her daughter replied, "I thought the tree would just shed its branches naturally." The mother chuckled and said, "They do..."

That's how I look at evolution. Yes, it is going to happen naturally, but if we put our attention on it we can do it gently... without breaking the windows.

It may seem silly, but have you asked yourself why "evolving" is in your best interest? It is probably at the core of why you picked up this book.

According to the Miriam-Webster dictionary, evolution is defined as "a process of change in a certain direction," and in the biological sense, it is "the process by which new species or populations of living things develop from preexisting forms through successive generations."

Indeed, evolution is a process of change over time. Living creatures evolve as a result of two combined factors: their environment and their habitual response to it.

We have been evolving since the first human decided to pick up stones as tools or cook his food over the newly discovered fire. Later, people began cultivating crops nearby instead of seeking food in the wild. Little by little, day by day, we evolve. Children evolve from curiosity and wonder.

So, "Why?" We evolve because we have wants. We wanted shelter. We wanted food. So we solved that by discovering caves and then building shelters. And then when we were comfortable, we started wanting safety and community. Then systems. Then success, artistic expression, and happiness. We want peace. Those wants are the engines behind evolution.

Evolution occurs whether we want it to or not, and whether we are aware of it or not. It has the potential to change for the better and to change for the worse; just as muscles evolve to become weaker or stronger depending on the forces acting upon them. It is influenced by all that we do and don't do, and all that we are and are not. Whether we are aware of it or not, we have a lot to do with how evolution unfolds. Therefore, it is in our best interest to practice conscious evolution while we are here on Earth.

For all of life's 13.7 billion years of cosmic, planetary, and biological evolution, we are on the leading edge of the evolutionary process. We represent the universe's newest self-discovery; its latest work of art.

Evolution has given us a special kind of consciousness, one that creates—and is thoroughly conditioned by—our languages, cultures, stories, and built environments. This consciousness and its companion social systems and technologies have awesome power to shape the world. We are just beginning to grow into a mature way of manifesting in the world.

Part of that maturing process is learning the dynamics through which evolution does its transformational work. Understanding those dynamics, we can apply them to transform ourselves.

In the classic movie, The Wizard of Oz, a group of characters are seeking help from a wise wizard. One character is a scarecrow seeking a brain, another is seeking a heart, and a third is seeking courage. When the characters finally meet the Wizard, they aren't imbued with courage, the compassion of a heart, nor the intellect of a brain. The characters simply shift their perspective to begin viewing themselves differently. Their views of themselves were challenged, then upgraded. As a result, I imagine their lives from that point on would unfold differently. The Scarecrow would begin to speak up more, the Tinman would show compassion, and the Lion would take chances—thereby changing their lives.

To the extent we do this, we are a facet of evolution that is becoming conscious of itself. Across many domains of society, life and spirituality, we are in the process of birthing ourselves as conscious evolution.

The crises of our age are manifestations of our challenge to consciously evolve. Co-intelligent conversation and democracy are fundamental to successfully transforming these crises into evolutionary breakthroughs.

A generation raised on "Don't drink and drive" invented Uber. Just as women raised with the idea that "Rosie the Riveter can do it!" sparked the feminist movement. First they began to believe that they could and then collectively they began to convince others. Or after watching movies like the Matrix, Parkour was invented and surged in popularity.

Those of us who are coming to understand and welcome this challenge to become conscious evolutionary agents discover new sources of inspiration and meaning in it—and find ourselves working as a community with truly remarkable companions as a result.

Conscious evolution is practiced through awareness, which leads to intention, and ultimately shapes our beliefs about who we are and what we are doing. From our beliefs, everything we are and will accomplish arises.

Intention is potential energy. When you pick up a pencil, for example, the action is first held in your mind as potential—your mind fully forms the action of reaching out and grasping, before you actually do.

Just as the intention of picking up a pencil unconsciously forms a blueprint for the action itself, so does adopting any intention, large or small. From picking up a pencil to changing your habits, your relationships, or your environment.

That is what makes belief so powerful.

What is Belief?

Belief works like a dam, except imagine that instead of water, the dam holds energy back; stored where it would otherwise flow freely. As the energy builds and builds with nowhere to go, it seems less and less possible to remove the dam; it starts to feel like an integral part of the environment. So when the dam is removed, the energy stored behind it becomes chaotic and turbulent, rushing forth unchecked. It forms new paths; you need more support to manage the environment while it adapts and changes to the release of energy.

Belief is a polarizing force. It attracts objects, people, and circumstances while repelling others, in alignment with the belief. When a person believes something, they not only align themselves and their actions with that belief, but something else more curious occurs: the belief aligns to them.

Belief creates vision. Belief creates strength of will. Belief creates resilience. Belief ignites and activates. Belief sees the invisible. It sees what has not yet been accomplished. Belief sees the goal, and it sees the path required to achieve the goal.

For instance, the belief "I am capable" would support us in taking on projects, setting goals, and reaching them. We hold some beliefs that work against us. They may have worked for you at a certain time, then circumstances changed— but the belief stayed. Another example: we may have learned as a child that it was safer to keep quiet. Then when we want to make a speech, or give a presentation, we get nervous because deep down we fear it still isn't safe.

A belief is a concept that you fully embrace and defend without doubting its validity. In fact, when you hold a belief, you seek evidence that the belief is true, thereby corkscrewing the belief deeper. To continue the example of public speaking, while we hold the belief that we are not safe to express ourselves we will draw in criticism that might make us feel unsafe. If we were to question and even reverse the belief that it is safer to express ourselves, we can make an impact by speaking out. The belief is what draws in the outcome. Taking some time to find what your subconscious beliefs are and changing them can change your life.

We usually don't want to look at the beliefs because they originate from a painful or scary event. We took on the belief to protect ourselves. When we recognize that a belief is no longer working for us, that is the exact time to reverse the belief. It will now be safe to process through the energy to uncover the belief. Although some beliefs dissipate with just the realization.

Think of it like pulling a fruit from a tree. When the fruit is ripe and ready to go, it can be effortless to pluck it off. But when it's a little too soon, where the fruit hasn't ripened enough, you'll meet significant resistance in pulling it off.

EVERYTHING IS AN ILLUSION

"Reality is an illusion, albeit a very persistent one."

-Albert Einstein

If you find yourself struggling to retain positive feelings or real belief about your intended outcome because your current "reality" seems far removed from it, remember that everything is an illusion. Your reality, the one you experience during your waking hours, is an illusion created by your dominant thoughts and beliefs and interpreted through your five physical senses. Yes, it is "real" in a physical sense, but in a non-physical sense it is no more real than the reality you wish to experience. This is because everything in the physical realm, whether wanted or unwanted, has its origin in the mental realm and hence, is subject to change through mental activity.

By consciously shaping your beliefs, you not only can but will transform your quality of life. Not only that, but you will learn and grow in ways you perhaps hadn't envisioned.

Have you noticed a pattern in the things you have succeeded at doing? The determining factor is belief—we only succeed when we BELIEVE we will succeed. And in accordance, we fail when we adopt the belief that failure will be the outcome. That without fail is THE only determining factor as to whether you are able to accomplish a thing or not.

Regardless of the size or scope of the event or circumstance being considered and regardless of who you are, what country you may live in, or what your religious preference might be, the Power of Belief... specifically the Power of YOUR belief, is behind it all.

It is due to the Power of Belief (or non-belief) which causes ANY condition, event, or circumstance you experience to manifest—and its outcome is only dependent on whether you believe that the thing can or can't manifest.

I remember my mom talking about her neighborhood. She didn't have many friends in the area, and she mentioned that the town was not inclusive. She felt that she didn't belong, and since they weren't welcoming she didn't try to get to know any neighbors. One day when we were driving through the neighborhood she started to tell me when people moved into each house. All of a sudden it dawned on her that she had been there the longest. After a long pause, she realized that she was the "old establishment" that hadn't been welcoming to them. It didn't take long for her to know the name of every neighbor and their dog, and soon afterward knew their stories. The belief that she didn't belong had been dissolved and without the belief there was nothing stopping her from befriending them. The actions of the neighbors hadn't changed; what changed was my mom's perspective, which in turn changed her behavior. Without the belief, she was free to act how she wished.

Successful performers, such as musicians and actors, often don't have a "plan B" or a backup career. If they did, they might have given up sooner and taken that other option. It's the moments where you believe you can give up, that you might....

It's the same when I was divorcing. If I felt like I couldn't make it on my own, I would have given up and perhaps gone back to the old relationship out of fear. Or, when I was learning to ride a bicycle, I thought I needed my mom's hand on the back of my bike. Then, after going a half a block, I noticed she wasn't with me and I immediately fell over. I believed that I couldn't do it without her. It was right then that the belief I needed her was dissipated—so I got back on the bike and rode on my own with confidence.

Awareness of Our Own Beliefs

Our beliefs create the values that we live our lives by.

It is important to know what your beliefs are, where they come from, and how to repair them if they are misaligned with what you want in life.

Our perceptions of the world, others, and of ourselves stem from our beliefs, which may have been formed long ago and have become outdated or corrupt. Even though we are adults and feel that we are now in control of our minds, the beliefs that were instilled in us as children and the negative reinforcements we have experienced and absorbed can still play a strong part in who we are, how we act and ultimately the results we obtain from life.

We all want to be able to blame someone or something else for our faults, shortcomings and failures; but the truth often is, it is we who are subconsciously sabotaging ourselves. There is no one to blame but our own unconscious selves.

Your thoughts are more powerful than you think; they impact everything in your daily life and have the potential to bring you many miseries—but also many joys.

You can achieve anything that you put your mind to, but your mind must first believe that that is true and to do that you may need to reprogram it to eradicate all the negative clutter that has accumulated throughout the years.

For example:
Do you believe you will be successful?
Do you believe you will be happy?
Do you truly believe that you can have what you want in life?

These are just popular beliefs. But they are productive ones nonetheless—by focusing on these, you will eventually reveal the negative beliefs that prevent them from being reality.

In the same way you continually maintain awareness of your physical self in order to be productive and fruitful in life's endeavors, awareness of your mind and heart will help you to recognize the beliefs that shape your life.

If you feel that you are not worthy of something, you will probably not get it. If you dwell on what you see as the negative aspects of your life, chances are you will never see the positive factors surrounding you.

Your brain is very capable of change; you can tap into your inner power and strength to change your life at any time.

"Whether you think you can or you think you can't—you're right."

-Henry Ford

You are in charge of your own fate and hold the key to the future you want and deserve. Just as the fundamentals of physics maintain that for every action there is a reaction, your brain, your life, and your future are subject to those very same fundamentals. If you believe in something and your thoughts are aligned to making it happen, then it will happen.

There are many great tools to aid in reprogramming your thoughts, to help you to reinforce beliefs that serve you and the others in your life, and to build on your awareness of how you affect and are affected by your own beliefs and those held by people close to you.

There is no greater power than belief, the belief in the power of your spirit and its ability to manifest whatever you need it to.

"Belief" by John Mayer

Is there anyone who

Ever remembers changing their mind from

The paint on a sign

Is there anyone who really recalls

Ever breaking rank at all

For something someone yelled real loud one time

Oh everyone believes

In how they think it ought to be

Oh everyone believes

And they're not going easily

2. Identity

Identity is not a determination of who or what you are; no more than a sweater or shoes are an integral part of your appearance. They are, instead, useful, interchangeable tools.

Identity is how you see yourself. Are you kind, smart, funny, or forgiving? These all sound like good traits, yet they will work against you in the moments where you are unkind, or make a mistake, or a joke falls flat, or you aren't ready to forgive someone. In these situations the identity is working against you. You will reject that part of you that is unkind and admonish yourself for not fitting into your identity. Your mind will seek out reasons and things to blame so that you can justify why you stepped out of your identity.

Your identity can be fluid like these traits or extend to attributes that are more solid. These seem and sometimes are more set for your journey. Are you a mother? Father? Biker? Knitter? These are names of different identities. While some identities feel thrust upon us at times, such as "Black," "White," "Japanese," "Canadian," "British," or even negative ones like "Criminal," your identities are entirely your choice. They can be adopted, swapped, or dropped at will. Think of how easily identities like "tourist" or "guest" are adopted and subsequently dropped when they cease to be useful.

There would be no use for identifying as a "tourist" when one comes back to their home—that identity was only useful as social "armor" in a foreign place; it allows others to excuse you for acting strangely or misunderstandings that arise according to the local culture.

Thus it is natural and easy to shift identities. The big question that many ask about identity: is there an authentic identity? In other words, is there an essential self and therefore an essential identity? There must be, for identity to be interchangeable by nature. Similarly, you can change your clothes with ease, but not your skin, which is integral to your body.

Physical traits and identity are independent of one another; beliefs around these traits, however, shape the identities we create around them. For example, "Short" is a physical characteristic that gives rise to an identity. This identity is adjusted constantly based on the expectations others have surrounding that identity and other factors that have shaped the individual's beliefs about what it means to be "Short" in society.

Identity is the mask we put on for others. Essence is what we are in our core; the quiet place in our minds. It contains the qualities we had when we were born, and those that will still live in us when we die. It includes basic human traits like love and goodness; authenticity, trust, creativity, and purpose. Identities, however, often include and incorporate concepts like fear, image, skepticism and suspicion, rigidity, and narrow-mindedness.

Identities form a continuum. We move up and down the continuum all day long. Around some people we feel safer and naturally closer to our essence; we don't feel the need for elaborate or complex identities. But around others we feel judged and present a different mask. Identities defend the part of us that has learned to self-protect and not let others in.

It is instinctive to raise up walls, and takes intention to lower them and bring up our essence.

An exercise to see how each identity feels is to remember a time when you weren't happy with the situation. Who was in the scene? What were they doing; what were you doing? Then notice how you feel physically. Stand up and shake it off to reset. And then call to mind someone or something that you know you love without a doubt. A baby, a pet, something that only feels wonderful. What about them makes you happy. Then pause and see how you are physically feeling. You will then have an idea of what living in your Essence feels like as opposed to living in an identity.

Identity is a specific mask we put on that does work for us when we take it on, and then it starts to hold us back. Motherhood; student, boss, woman, engineer, American, vegetarian, athlete. As you can see these aren't bad things, they just limit us when clung to, and when they start to define us and we derive our personal value from them, it can become more toxic.

The identity of being beautiful might sound like a nice one to have. Feeling beautiful might grant you confidence in yourself. You might feel more able to enter a room and talk to people; or during a job interview it might make it easier to communicate your positive attributes. While it can work for you, it might also work against you when your hair isn't done right, or you are in pajamas at the grocery store. The confidence that depends on the identity is fickle and unforgiving. As you age, you might be resisting how your looks are changing more because of the loss of the confidence and self assuredness than of the actual looks. Realizing that can help you find a source that is more perpetual and consistent.

While they can be detrimental in practice, when kept past their usefulness, identities aren't inherently bad or false. They help us take on challenges, and that's what they're for. To be mindful of our identities, however, we need to examine the beliefs that surround them. Beliefs shape identity; not all are adopted consciously, and some are no longer necessary.

The most powerful identity I have identified and softened is motherhood. Being a good mother has helped me prioritize my children. I am not exaggerating to say without it, my children might not be alive. We feed and nurture our children and it is driven by love underneath, as all identities are, and it helped me find value in myself after giving up my career which had been my source of value before motherhood. However, now that they have grown into adults, trying to "mother" them can have a detrimental impact on our new adult/adult relationship. It can make an adult child feel not good enough, or inadequate and create resentment. If I am still finding value in motherhood then if they make a choice that doesn't reflect well on my image of how things are supposed to be, then I am motivated to try to correct it. So that I can feel fulfilled as a mother, and feed into that identity. But if I allow myself to feel value and fulfillment from other sources then the adult children are free to walk their own path. This is not new. This is the process of becoming empty nesters. This process of letting go and reconnecting with yourself is completing an identity life-cycle. It works for you until it begins not to. Once it is no longer working for you, that is the moment to release it.

Identities are often multi-layered and cannot exist without multiple people participating. These can be as niche and minute as "Sunni" or "Methodist," to wide-reaching, such as "South African," "Human," "Living Being," or "Spirit."

In a way, all of these identities are expressions of our essence, or spirit. Your spirit navigates much of its life here on Earth by adopting various identities, while in truth, your spirit is able to experience any and all identities, should it choose to. Thus, the essential "you," your spirit, is both none of the identities it takes on and all of them at once. Identity is how we live the larger story and the smaller stories that make up this life, the lives to come, and those that came before.

So when an identity holds us back, we must examine the beliefs that gave rise to that identity.

Try testing one of the identities you hold. Ask yourself:

Why did I choose to adopt this identity?

What challenge or circumstances made this identity important for me?

How does this identity still serve me?

What beliefs am I holding that prevent me from letting it go?

If I no longer used this identity, how would my life be different?

How would I change? How would the people around me change?

Every time you discover you are using an identity, ask these questions again. Make a list with two columns: one of the identities that are still helping you, and one of those no longer helping you. Envision how you might be with only those useful identities.

Following the example of motherhood and empty nester, with these questions, you can find what you were getting as a result of being a "good mother." The identity may have been the source of self value, or it may have been the technique of expressing unconditional love that no longer has a recipient. Your mind might be telling you that it is the only way to express that energy, or that you are no longer useful, but recognizing the purpose of the identity can be a helpful tool. Because there are infinite ways to create the feelings one may have gotten from being a mother. Releasing the identity opens up more ways to feel valuable or love, or whatever feeling you had been feeling. Taking time to connect with yourself, your spirit, that inner voice can guide you to whatever follows. For me it was an opening to a larger community. One that includes my adult children, but without placing an unwritten burden on them to help me feel fulfilled.

Perhaps you don't need to identify as a "victim," or "depressed" or "lonely" anymore—or maybe "mother" and "hard worker" are getting in each other's way. Working to understand and clear the beliefs surrounding your unhelpful identities will open your consciousness to new creative possibilities neither you or anyone else has envisioned before.

"We who look at the whole and not just the part, know that we too are systems of interdependence, of feelings, perceptions, thoughts, and consciousness all interconnected. Investigating in this way, we come to realize that there is no 'me' or 'mine' in any one part, just as a sound does not belong to any one part of the lute."

-Buddha, from Samyutta Nikaya

3. Vibration

Everything in the Universe is energy. This was the conceptual breakthrough made by German physicist Albert Einstein which generated the famous equation, $E=mc^2$. Essentially, it showed that there was a concrete mathematical relationship between matter and energy—implying that matter IS energy, in incredibly dense form.

It turns out that matter is just energy that vibrates at a certain frequency; just as water can be a gas at high temperature (higher energy), a liquid at medium temperature, and solid at low temperature (lower energy).

We can think of consciousness in the same way. Different thoughts, and thought patterns, also carry vibration. Lower vibrational thoughts, such as the thought "I am hungry" barely resonate through your consciousness, while a thought like "Should I apologize?" vibrates much higher, having many layers and possible implications.

Consciousness can, thus, be dissected into "layers" or degrees, just as the different states of matter (such as solid, liquid, gas) describe the vibration of physical particles. However, there is no physical separation between any two degrees of consciousness, because consciousness is unconstrained by space and time.

Vibration is protean. It is not the source of any energy or power by itself; it is rather a result of power; just as the notes of a guitar reaching your ears are actually the resonating vibrations created by a skilled finger precisely plucking the strings.

VIBRATIONAL MANAGEMENT

As conscious beings, we are able to manage the vibrations we receive through mindfulness.

We "practice" mindfulness so we can learn how to recognize when our minds are doing their normal everyday work and take pause for a while so we can choose what we'd like to focus on. In a nutshell, mindfulness helps us have a much healthier relationship with ourselves (and, by extension, with others).

MEDITATION

We use the word meditation to mean many things. But simply put, it is resting your brain. Literally any moment without thought can be meditation. There are moments and environments where it is easier to do than others. Since meditation comes to us from Eastern cultures, we tend to imagine that the only way is to sit like the Buddha and chant. But meditation can take many forms. The idea is to sit in a way where the body doesn't distract from your goal of non-thought. So, find a comfortable way to sit and relax.

Once in that setting, begin to focus your mind on something. Breath for me is the simplest because it is always with me. The reason they chant is because it helps keep your mind from producing a thought. As an exercise, first take a moment to pay attention to your body before you begin. Notice where you are tight and where you feel tension—where do you feel more dense and heavy? Then read through the exercise and note again how you are feeling. Just the act of meditation can help you feel lighter and more connected with yourself. You might want to record yourself and then play it back to allow yourself to fully surrender into relaxation. If you do choose to record yourself, include pauses. If not, then allow yourself to relax and set a timer with a gentle alarm to bring you back. This is so you can fully relax and not worry about time. You can begin with as little as a minute if that's all you can do. Each time, you can extend the length. The more you do it, the more you will be able to do it.

Notice where your body is supported. Are you sitting? Laying? Standing? Where do you feel the support underneath you? Where is the earth supporting you? Then allow it to support you a little more. Notice where you are holding on and see if you can let yourself let go. There is always another layer to release. If you feel comfortable, close your eyes. Then bring your focus to your breath. Notice that it is cool when breathing in, and warm when breathing out. As thoughts enter your mind, recognize them as a thought, and release them and bring your attention back to your breath.

When you are ready to end your meditation, bring your attention back to your body. Wiggle fingers and toes, open your eyes. Draw your attention to your body. Are you more relaxed afterwards?

I have found that if I am trying to force a task, I can find myself working on it for hours. Yet if I would take even a 5 minute meditation, I can more easily complete the task in a fraction of the time. So it is not only good for your mind and body, it can help your productivity. Meditation raises your vibration as well.

Managing our vibrations is a process of balancing our body & mind's responses to the energies acting on us. Meditation is a practice where an individual uses a technique – such as mindfulness, or focusing the mind on a particular object, thought, or activity – to train attention and awareness, and achieve a mentally clear and emotionally calm and stable state. While there are countless seminars, workshops, gurus, yogis, and teachers who all espouse some form of meditation, the basic concept of meditation (and most important take-away) is surrender.

WHAT IS CONSCIOUSNESS?

Put most simply, consciousness is living awareness. Our expression of consciousness is tied to our concept of self: the more limited the sense of self, the smaller threshold we have for experience. Thus, culturally inherited or otherwise adopted beliefs have limiting effects on both our individual consciousness as well as our collective consciousness.

Lower degrees of consciousness are physically denser and hence more accessible to our physical senses. Higher degrees of consciousness vibrate at higher frequencies and (similar to a dog whistle), are subtler and less accessible to our physical senses. Indeed, the higher the degree of consciousness of a thing or concept, then the more positive it is on the Scale of Consciousness. In turn, higher positivity corresponds to higher levels of self-awareness, ability to pay attention intelligently, and the capacity to willingly manifest.

Looked at another way, the lowest or densest rates of vibration of consciousness in the physical world are found in inanimate objects, which may be alive with consciousness but have no self-awareness or conscious intelligence. In contrast, the most powerful human beings, who are able to influence all things and people in their environment effortlessly, have carefully cultivated higher patterns of thought through examining and releasing limiting beliefs.

Indeed, it is humanity's degree of self-aware consciousness, and hence our capacity to use Intention to mentally direct ourselves that allows us to experience higher vibrational energies if we choose. It also distinguishes one human being from another. Put simply, while everything is alive with consciousness, not everything lives consciously. Unless you are intentionally focusing your energy and consciousness as a lifestyle, you might as well be living unconsciously.

Higher degrees of consciousness correspond to higher degrees of conscious use of intention. Moreover, higher degrees of intention are associated with the power to direct change in those things of a relatively lower degree of consciousness. In other words, the higher the degree of consciousness of a thing then the greater its power to willingly direct change in all those things of a lower degree of consciousness. Power in this sense, however, does not suggest force or physical amounts of power. In contrast, it means directive power in the absence of physical force, or in other words, the power to direct change in things at a lesser vibration.

A vibration emanating from someone isn't necessarily their permanent vibration and is unchangeable. It is fluid, can rise and fall, and your vibration will have an impact on theirs.

Once I was in an argument with someone over the phone. I was heading to them in the car. The argument had triggered me into a lower vibration. I decided to end the conversation for the few minutes remaining in my trip. I pulled over to sit in a park for a few minutes. I cried, and felt and breathed and did all of the stuff that I am suggesting in this book. I discovered the belief that had been triggered in the phone conversation. Once released, I felt at peace and full of love for the person who I had just been arguing with. When I walked in, and looked at this person with soft love in my eyes, and felt at peace, his vibration was affected. After that moment, using my scientific mind I did an experiment.

The next time he was upset and raising his voice, I called to mind a moment when I felt love for him. I let the love swell in my heart as he was continuing. Then when the feeling became too intense, I imagined sending that energy towards him and enveloping him in it. He literally stopped yelling at me, and asked "What was I just saying?" His frustration with me at that moment had been rooted in fear. I didn't need to know what it was. I simply sent my higher-vibration energy (in that moment) towards him and his vibration was raised. He was then able to calmly explain his perspective.

Everything in the universe is made up of molecules vibrating at different speeds. This includes trees, bodies, rocks, animals, thoughts, and emotions. Human vibrations are composed of everything from physical matter to the way you communicate the thoughts you think. In simple terms, some molecules vibrate faster and some vibrate slower; there are higher vibrations and lower vibrations. Vibrational patterns include the frequencies of things like radio waves, sound, and light.

When you are vibrating at a higher level, you feel lighter, happier, and more at ease, while lower vibrations feel heavy, dark, and confused. Almost all spiritual traditions point the way toward higher realms of consciousness and vibration, and scientific studies (like that of the author Dr. David Hawkins) have even quantified the vibrations of different states of being to create a scale of consciousness.

Rock Bottom: Shame

The level of Shame is close to death, which may be chosen out of Shame. This can be overt, like suicide, or subtly chosen by failure to take steps to prolong life. Death by avoidable accident is common. We all have some awareness of the pain of embarrassment, being discredited, or feeling like a "nonperson." In Shame, people hang their heads and slink away, wishing they were invisible. Banishment is a traditional way of ultimately shaming someone; in more primitive times banishment was equivalent to death. Early life experiences such as sexual abuse, which lead to Shame, warp us; often for a lifetime unless these issues are resolved. Shame is destructive to emotional and psychological health and as a consequence of low self-esteem, makes development of physical illness more likely. Personalities carrying Shame tend to be shy, withdrawn, and introverted.

The Central Anchor: Love

Love is a bit of an overstated concept. What culture generally refers to as "love" is an intense emotional and physical sensation. It is usually fluid and fluctuating, waxing and waning with varying conditions. When frustrated, this sensation often reveals an underlying anger and dependency. That love can turn to hate is often supposed, but Hate stems from Pride, not Love.

Love that is unconditional and unchanging. It does not fluctuate because its source within the person who loves is not dependent on external conditions. Loving is a state of being. It is a way of relating to the world that is forgiving, nurturing, and supportive. Love is not intellectual and does not proceed from the mind. Love emanates from the heart. It has the capacity to lift others and accomplish great feats because of its purity of motive.

Pure Consciousness

Yes, even higher than love is is the level of the "Great Ones" of history, who originated the spiritual patterns that multitudes have followed throughout history. All are associated with Divinity, and it is certainly a level of powerful inspiration. At this level, there is no longer an individual self separate from others; rather, there is an identification of Self with a larger consciousness and divinity.

This transcendence of ego also serves by example to teach others how it can be accomplished. This is the peak of the evolution of consciousness in human form. Great teachings uplift the masses and raise the level of awareness of all of humanity. To have such vision is called "grace," and the gift it brings is infinite peace. At this level of realization, the sense of one's existence transcends all time and all individuality. There is no longer any identification with the physical body as "me," and therefore, its fate is of no concern. The body is seen as merely a tool of consciousness through the intervention of the mind, its prime value that of communication. The self merges back into the Self. This is the level of nonduality, or complete Oneness. There is no localization of consciousness; awareness is everywhere and equally present.

The Power of Creativity

Creativity and genius are the center of powerful higher vibrations. Human history is the record of man's struggle to comprehend truths which to those of genius appear obvious. Genius is by definition a style of consciousness characterized by the ability to access higher vibrations. It is not a personality characteristic. It is not something that a person "has," or even something that someone "is." Those in whom we recognize genius commonly disclaim it. A universal characteristic of genius is humility. The genius has always attributed his insights to some higher influence.

The great works of art, music, and architecture that have come down to us through the centuries are enduring representations of the effect of high-energy vibrations. In them, we see a reflection of the commitment of the master artists of our civilization to perfection and grace, and thereby to the ennoblement of all humanity.

Higher vibrational patterns have specific resonances; as do musical tones. The higher the vibrational frequency, the higher the power. What the genius arrives at is a new vibration. Every advance in human consciousness has come through a leap from a lower vibration to a higher vibration.

Thus, creative genius is not only an achievable pattern of consciousness, but one that exists in a form unique and unmatched in each individual person. Unlocking it is a straightforward process: of first Understanding, then of Acting, then of Being.

4. Chakras and Energy Layers

What are Chakras?

Physically, chakras are clusters of nerves in our body. Years before we knew what nerve endings were, spiritually these areas had meaning. The word Chakra means wheel, so they initially saw them as energy focal points that turned like wheels. There are seven major ones along our spine that most people mean when they refer to chakras, although there are more than a hundred in our body. The seven aforementioned regulate the energy systems in our body. I see it as a road map. We have major highways and minor roadways that feed into them. These seven would be the major intersections where energy follows different pathways.

These intersections or clusters can become congested or free flowing. They can even become too open. Just like in the middle of the night, I can hear cars racing down the empty road by my house, it's not always the safest situation to have it too open. Our goal is to have these seven balanced.

There are many techniques to balance the chakras. Some become too open, compensating for those that have closed. Many times two or three chakras work together that often compensate for each other's off balanced condition. Following the road metaphor, when a road becomes too congested drivers will seek alternate routes. This may have a negative impact on a neighborhood street, so it is a good goal to keep all the roads flowing.

Keeping a chakra open is a bit more of a challenge, but not so difficult when you have awareness. Since mind, body, soul, and spirit are all intertwined, awareness of an imbalance in one area through chakra meditation will help bring the others back into balance.

There is a correlation with each chakra to a physical system in the human body. Each chakra governs different systems. When that chakra is out of balance, over time, we can develop physical symptoms. In this time we are living in, we need to address both the physical symptom and the energetic cause behind it. As you treat the disease you also heal the imbalance.

Take for example: a person mourning a loss who subsequently develops bronchitis. This disease manifests in the chest, causing chest pains and coughing. In this case, the heart chakra is radiating negative energy outward, manifesting the disease. However, if this person realizes the connection between the loss and the disease, healing will occur much faster if she honors the grieving process and treats it along with the physical ailment.

THE CHAKRAS

The first three chakras, starting at the base of the spine, are "chakras of matter." They are the most physical in nature.

1. Root Chakra

The Root is the chakra of stability, security, and our basic needs. It encompasses the first three vertebrae, the bladder, and the colon. When this chakra is open, we feel safe and fearless. When closed we feel unsupported, worry about lack, and resentment towards those who appear supported and abundant.

The Root chakra is about being physically a member of a community and feeling at home in situations. When it is open, you feel more grounded, stable and secure. You feel that people are trustworthy in general. You feel present in the here and now and connected to your physical body. You feel you have sufficient territory.

If you tend to be fearful or nervous, your Root Chakra is probably underactive. You'd easily feel unwelcome.

If this chakra is overactive, you may be very materialistic and greedy. You're probably obsessed with being secure and you may resist change.

2. Sacral Chakra

This chakra is our creativity and sexual center. It is located above the pubic bone, below the navel, and is responsible for our creative genesis.

The Sacral chakra is about feeling and sexuality. When it is open, your feelings flow freely, and are expressed without you being over-emotional. You are open to intimacy and you can be passionate and lively. You have no problems dealing with your sexuality.

If you tend to be stiff and unemotional or have a "poker face," the Sacral chakra is under-active. You're not very open to people.

If this chakra is overactive, you tend to be emotional all the time. You'll feel emotionally attached to people and you can be overly sexual.

Balancing a given chakra is akin to a pendulum— you can fluctuate between the chakra's two extremes. The whole spectrum of chakras also has a natural "swing" of energy; a lower chakra being closed, for example, is like a kinked hose; the flow of energy between seemingly unaffected chakras will be hindered. Remember that creativity flows through you from the Sacral Chakra upwards; which is why, as creators, it is so important to balance our chakras.

3. Navel Chakra

This chakra is located in the area from the navel to the breastbone. The third chakra is our source of personal power. In addition, this is sometimes called the "solar plexus chakra."

When the Navel Chakra is under-active, you tend to be passive and indecisive. You're probably timid and don't get what you want— and likely blame others. This chakra tends to be where we hold beliefs that deal with our personal (in)capabilities.

The Navel Chakra contains the energy center that regulates your metabolism. Your self-image and beliefs thereto are held in this area, and will affect how your body regulates energy.

When this chakra is balanced, you feel confident, capable, and fearless. You face conflict with grace, and you no longer experience doubts about yourself and your capacities.

If this chakra is overactive, you are more prone to being domineering and even aggressive.

4. Heart Chakra

Located at the center, the fourth chakra, is at the middle of the seven and unites the lower chakras of matter and the upper chakras of spirit. The fourth is also spiritual but serves as a bridge between our body, mind, emotions, and spirit. The heart chakra is our source of love and connection.

When we work through our physical chakras, or the first three, we can open the spiritual chakras more fully.

The Heart chakra is about love, kindness and affection. When it is open, you are compassionate and friendly, and you work at harmonious relationships.

When your Heart chakra is underactive, you are more cold and distant.

If this chakra is overactive, you may be suffocating people with your love and your love is likely serving as a subconscious salve for some kind of pain you are experiencing.

5. Throat Chakra

The chakra is the fifth chakra, located in the area of the throat. This is our source of verbal expression and the ability to speak our highest truth. The fifth chakra includes the neck, thyroid, and parathyroid glands, jaw, mouth, and tongue.

The Throat chakra is about self-expression and talking. When it is open, you have no problems expressing yourself, and you might be doing so as an artist. Creativity that flows upward from the Sacral Chakra is ultimately expressed through the throat chakra, even if not through speech (think of how when you write, the part of your brain that forms words is also fully activated and working as if you were speaking. And this is true for many other creative activities as well).

When this chakra is under-active, you tend not to speak much (or you constantly 'edit' what you wish to say), and you probably are introverted and shy. Not speaking the truth may block this chakra.

If this chakra is overactive, you tend to speak too much, usually to dominate and keep people at a distance. Poor listening skills often accompany a blocked throat chakra.

6. Third Eye Chakra

The chakra is located in between the eyebrows. It is also referred to as the "third eye" chakra. It is our center of intuition. We all have a sense of intuition but we may not listen to or heed its messages.

This chakra is key to conscious manifestation, as it allows one to see what could be. Manifestation relies on focused intention combined with clear visualization through the third eye.

If it is under-active, you're not very good at thinking for yourself, and you may tend to rely on authorities. You may be rigid in your thinking, relying on beliefs too much. You might even get confused easily.

If this chakra is overactive, you may live in a world of fantasy too much. In excessive cases hallucinations are even possible. This is because energy moves through the human body, from chakra to chakra, like traffic. When we say a chakra is "over-active," you can think of it as simply harboring too much energy—sort of like an "energy traffic jam."

7. Crown Chakra

The Crown chakra is located at the crown of the head. This is the chakra of enlightenment and spiritual connection to our higher selves, others, and ultimately, to the divine.

If it is under-active, you're not very aware of spirituality. You're probably quite rigid in your thinking.

If this chakra is overactive, you are probably intellectualizing things too much. You may be "addicted to spirituality" and are probably ignoring your bodily needs.

This chakra is affected by what authorities you accept. For example, being in an abusive relationship will devastate the Crown Chakra; by accepting a malevolent authority (the abuser), this authority is then both literally and metaphorically "above" the chakra and preventing any connection to higher awareness. Conversely, a mutually supportive, loving and caring relationship will not be an obstacle, as it commands no authority, but rather arises naturally from below (the heart chakra) and actually facilitates better energy flow out of the Crown.

Awareness to which of your chakras are out of balance is key to aligning them. Our bodies are in constant flux between balance and imbalance. Unless you experience an apparent problem in one area of the body, imbalances can be difficult to detect. That being said, it's good to bring pure awareness to your body/mind and start understanding its signals and clues so that you can align your chakras.

For example, frequent constipation can indicate a blockage in the first chakra. A recurring sore throat leaves clues to a blocked fifth chakra. Frequent headaches around the area of the forehead may mean your sixth chakra is blocked.

The Chakras are as important to our health and well-being as the organ systems of our physical bodies. By practicing mindfulness of your Chakras, you can gain great insights about your life and the circumstances you find yourself in. For example, you can "test" the basis of a relationship using the Chakras by locating its center within your Chakras. A relationship that is centered in the Heart Chakra will find its basis in love, and is the type of relationship people mean when they say "true love." But a relationship centered in the Sacral Chakra may be full of creative and sexual energy, but lack true depth and connection.

For more information on Chakras and how they affect our lives and bodies, the book Anatomy of the Spirit by Caroline Myss is a must-read.

The Layers of Human Energy

Just as light can be divided into the different colors of a rainbow with a prism, the human's soul can be separated into different layers. And just as without a prism it is one light, whole and complete. Looking at the different layers we can understand ourselves a little more. Why are some things easier to change about ourselves where others are much more ingrained and we can find ourselves repeating an unwanted pattern. It could be because we hold some habits, beliefs, or self images in some of the more subtle or outer layers of the soul.

We, as humans, are conduits for energy. Energy is both moving through us and coalescing within our bodies. Just as a radio tower emanates energy in the form of radio waves and a television emanates energy in the form of light waves that are then seen by the eye, the human body is both a receiver and a transmitter of its own unique energy field.

People have known about, measured, and studied human energy fields for thousands of years, particularly in Hindu and Buddhist circles. In the Bhagavad Gita, which is one of the Hindu sacred texts, the "subtle body" is described as a combination of the mind, the intellect and the ego, and it is the subtle body that controls the physical body.

The Causal Body field extends to around 9 feet, while the Subtle Body extends around 3 inches outward around the physical body. Have you ever sensed that someone was looking at you, then proved yourself right in the next instant? Or sensed someone enter the room, without seeing or hearing them? These common experiences are sensory interactions with human energy fields.

Thus, in order from least dense to most dense, the causal body -> the subtle body -> the physical body.

All three bodies are interconnected, and optimal living occurs when they are in harmony with one another. It is believed that the subtle body transmigrates (along with the causal) after physical death, operating as a medium for reincarnation (in other words, it is an aspect of the 'soul').

Although it cannot be seen with the physical eye, energetic awareness can be developed through the "third eye," or spiritual awareness. Moving outwards from the physical body, each energy layer vibrates at a faster rate than the one before it.

Each layer of energy, moving outwards, encapsulates the others; similar to a matryoshka doll, which if you aren't familiar, is a traditionally Russian trinket in the shape of a little lady which contains another slightly smaller lady, which in turn contains another slightly smaller lady, and so on and so forth until you reach the smallest (but densest) version of her.

As awareness of each body develops, one moves closer to understanding of the true Self, and strengthens the connection with universal energy, or God.

Any blockage or imbalance within this system can cause physical and mental discomfort, illness and disease. In traditional Indian and Tibetan medicine, the subtle body model is used as a map of the central nervous system's function in order to diagnose and treat ailments.

ADDITIONAL SUB-LAYERS

The "bodies of energy" can be further subdivided based on individual chakral energy. Each chakra exchanges energy with every other one, forming a kind of "frequency" layer emanating from that particular chakra. By peeling back each layer, we can begin to understand and identify where problems in our bodies and in our lives are coming from. From densest to least dense, they are:

The Etheric Body

Everything that exists in the physical plane has its own etheric body counterpart. The human etheric body is the vibrating web of energy from which our energetic blueprint is created. It is the densest non-physical layer. Vibrating at a slightly higher frequency than the physical plane it is normally unseen but nonetheless important for our well-being. Its strength & vitality can be undermined by shock, trauma & drug use as well as unresolved issues filtering down to it from other layers. The etheric body is linked to the root chakra.

The Emotional Body

The emotional memories and patterns that are stored in our emotional body trigger our emotional responses to the events in our lives. The emotional body is the layer of energy beyond the etheric body and is unique to each individual. It contains all our emotions and feelings including those created by unresolved issues from other life times.

The emotional body functions outside of third dimensional reality and so has no recognition of time. This is why sometimes a person's emotional reaction to a particular situation can seem completely out of proportion to what is currently happening in their lives. The trigger in fact comes from a previous unresolved trauma. These emotional responses are brought into incarnation via the soul and mental bodies for resolution.

The emotional body is linked to the sacral chakra. Emotional energy is very powerful as it gives power to our thoughts and intentions. Looking into a clear lake, even if there are no waves present, you can see the evidence of waves etched into the sand - the "memory," therefore, is preserved by the sand. Think of the emotional body as that "sand."

The Mental Body

The mental body receives, stores and transmits all our thought patterns and mental processes. It is linked to the solar plexus chakra. Thoughts extend beyond the mental body as energy and create our realities so it is important to choose the thoughts that we allow to dwell in our minds. When we link thought with the power of emotions we become creators so it is important to monitor that which we are choosing whether consciously or unconsciously.

The Egoic Body

The Egoic body is the layer of energy linked to the heart chakra and is therefore the bridge from the physical to the spiritual realms. When we maintain an open heart chakra we receive light, information and inspiration from our soul through the Egoic body. This layer of energy acts as a filter for past life information and karmic patterns to come into consciousness. Here we are starting to pass beyond the mind and logical understanding; the egoic body can be understood using both logical thinking and metaphorical thinking, but as we move into the higher bodies, they become increasingly difficult to conceptualize using purely logical thinking.

The Causal Body

The Causal body is the doorway to higher consciousness and links the personality to the collective consciousness of the planet. The causal body is the layer of energy beyond the egoic body and is linked to the throat chakra. The causal body can be seen energetically as containing everything that is real and permanent about us. Gifts and talents that you have attained in previous lives are sealed into your causal body and made available to you through your soul when you are ready to use them. Developing an awareness of your Causal Body and those that follow is more easily done through metaphorical thinking rather than purely logical thinking.

Many teachers, writers, and philosophers do teach with a purely logical approach to the higher layers, which some people find more natural for their minds. But many of us find that metaphorically approaching these concepts is more natural and graceful. If you feel discouraged, or you find these concepts logically difficult to understand, try using only metaphors.

For example, you would find it difficult—if not impossible—to describe color to a blind person using scientific definitions of wavelengths and photons. Using metaphor, such as describing how a color feels (like describing "blue" by placing ice in their hand) is not only more effective, but may open a door to a higher understanding of the concept of color.

The Soul Body

This body holds the essence of your spirit—the part of you that is of God. Inspiration and spiritual visions filter down to the soul to be grounded in the now through the lower chakras, allowing us to manifest divine will or the will of our spirit. This is linked to the third eye chakra.

The Soul Body is commonly accessed through meditation, and communicates with our lower bodies in the spaces between our thoughts, as its ideas transcend our thinking and physical brains.

The Integrated Spiritual Body

This level is the highest and purest form, in which all aspects of all the energetic layers as well as the physical are encapsulated. So this body contains all the integrated spiritual principles that an individual may work with. It is essentially the "whole" body (the 'outermost' layer), like all the layers of the matryoshka doll put together. This is linked to the Crown chakra.

THE COLLECTIVE BODIES

Every one of us is connected to everyone else. We are part of the fabric of existence; each of us is like a separate thread in the elegant tapestry of the universe. Where our energy fields merge with the larger fields of Humanity, of Earth, and of the larger Universe are focal points we can become aware of and tap into. While some experts and teachers describe dozens, or even hundreds of these focal points, to keep it understandable we will discuss a few of the most easily relatable ones.

Earth Star

This subtle energy point is about 9 inches below the feet in a direct line with the base chakra and hara point. The earth star is an important energy centre because it is our alignment point with the earth's magnetic grid and ensures that we are able to effectively ground and focus energy. Being properly grounded through the earth star is essential for us to fully connect with our multidimensional selves, the ascended realms and other star systems.

The Hara

The Hara is a subtle energy centre situated in the auric field just below the navel. It is not the same as the sacral chakra. Located in the center of the abdomen are the organs that give us life. In their very center we find the navel, which in many traditions is called Spirit Gate—it refers to the place where we received life from our mother through the umbilical cord. As such, these areas are the focal point of energy in our body from which life is given, sustained, and taken away.

When the hara point is working properly it brings forward an awareness of the need to follow divine will, promoting a sense of true purpose & fulfilment as well as a greater sense of being centred in the physical body. It resonates outward from the solar plexus chakra.

Thymus Point

An important subtle energy point that stimulates the development of unconditional love and compassion. The ancient spiritually attuned civilizations all had this energy point fully functioning and recognised its true purpose as the 'Higher Heart' centre or chakra point. A message to us of the importance of this centre in our unfolding spiritual development.

Soul Star

This subtle energy point is situated above the crown chakra and higher chakras. When activated it is aligned with the soul, all 'higher' energies, star systems and the universe, allowing a greater amount of soul energy, light, guidance and healing to filter through to the personality.

Consider this exercise: get physically comfortable and relax into whatever supports your body. Breathe in and imagine your energy resonating two inches outside of your body. Then allow it to expand to a few feet. Feel it fill the room until you can sense its corners. Let it go further until it fills the whole building, then beyond, into the atmosphere, filling the town and region you find yourself. Let it keep going, become lighter along with it as it surrounds the whole planet.

You'll find it will still expand, growing to encapsulate the whole solar system, even larger than the Sun, faster than the speed of light as it becomes larger and larger, encapsulating the galaxy and its 400 billion stars, until you can no longer even keep track of its size in your mind. Feel the energy as it becomes one with the infinite universe.

When you're ready, bring your awareness back to your body, your anchor. Whenever you feel heaviness, whether it be from life's burdens or just a dense, low-vibrational feeling, reach out once again to the lightness of being as large as the whole galaxy, or of the entire universe. Remember that your highest self is so light, not even space, time, or velocity matter to it.

Meditate on Your Chakras

Despite the unavoidably esoteric nature of energy fields, developing an awareness of their nature can be extremely beneficial. Unless you are a physicist, the chakras and energetic fields are not meant to be understood through purely mental, or conceptual means. We experience them intuitively—just as in the earlier example of being able to sense someone entering the room, or looking at you.

Start with the chakras. Calm your body and visualize each chakra one at a time. Sit or lie down somewhere comfortable. Develop an awareness of your tailbone, which supports your body when you sit or stand, at the base of your pelvis. Allow your body to rest even more upon it. Then allow it some more. Go again, into a deeper layer of rest upon this chakra. This is your Root Chakra, which connects you to the larger energy of the Earth. Feel its physical presence, and the grounding energy it encapsulates.

Move your awareness upwards, to your Sacral Chakra, which is located just above the pubic bone. Allow it to speak to you if it wants to—it is the source of creative energy in your body. It is full of energy and is only healthy when it is free.

Continue upwards to your Navel Chakra. Here is your metabolic center, regulating the glucose in your blood, feeding your brain and other organs. Breathe deeply and feel this chakra fill with oxygen. Without judgment, become aware of the beliefs about yourself you're holding in this area. Allow them to arise and take note of them, but don't react. It may be difficult at first, but becoming aware is the important first step in the work—it is already a loosening of your "grip" on these beliefs.

Once more, move upwards, feeling through your Heart Chakra. Once again, breathe deeply, and feel this chakra swell with oxygenated blood and energy. Listen to the emotions held here. Do you feel joy? Sadness? Excitement? Loneliness? Take note of how this emotional center feels, again, without judging. Here is where your spiritual energies (higher vibrations of lesser density) are resonating together with your physical energies (lower vibrations of higher density). Allow your awareness to completely encapsulate your heart and the area surrounding it. Allow the powerful love of the universe to rise to the top of your awareness.

Next is your Throat Chakra. Here is where the energy stored in your body can express itself as physical vibration in your vocal cords, creating the words you speak. Feel your breath passing through your throat on its way to your lungs. This chakra is not only the expressive center of the physical words you speak, but of all your creative energies. Become aware of the unspoken words living in this chakra—words "on the tip of your tongue." Instead of judging or jumping to express them, allow them to enter your awareness. As they fade, become aware of the other words and messages living there, but not demanding as much of your attention/energy. What does your spirit want to say? Perhaps there aren't specific words, but a large, passionate message, such as the desire to play music, write, paint, or create. You may want to write down what you experience while exploring this chakra.

As you move upwards, through your neck, the bones of your lower face and your sensitive tongue and nose, your awareness will come to rest on the anchor located just behind the top of your nose, between your eyebrows, in the center of your brain. This is the focal point of your entire nervous system, its control center—the Third Eye Chakra. Allow your thoughts and feelings here to flow freely, not judging whatever you find. Here is where your spirit already knows what you're reading and thoroughly understands it. This is your center of intention, of visualization, and manifestation. Here is where your creative energy, with its roots in your Sacral Chakra, is at the top of its stalk, where the flower of creation is budding.

The petals of this flower, sometimes called the "Thousand Petal Lotus," are the Crown Chakra. Here, at the very top of your head, the higher energies of the Universe are soaking in, like warm sunlight on the petals. Soften the Crown and let this warmth in. Trust in this higher energy and its purity. Mysterious and esoteric, it is not possible to understand with your mind, but rather, is to be experienced by your higher self. The Crown Chakra is like a cell phone that receives messages from a tower—the "antenna" which downloads the energy and creativity of the impossibly large and beautiful Universe.

Now that your chakras are more open, allow energy to naturally flow from the ground up, and feel it simultaneously flow from the top down. Bask in this flow, take note of how it feels, and return when you're ready to do so again. This exercise is a way to center and liberate the energy flowing through your body and spirit. Capture this feeling in your memory, and access it as needed. Even in circumstances when you don't have the time or environment to meditate, you can connect with this vibration you've created for yourself.

PART II: THE PAST

5. Heart Space

Meditation and visualization are powerful tools that when combined, can offer great insight into ourselves and allow us to not only more deeply explore our own inner being, but also make contact with and consult our Spirit Guides.

Exploring Deeper Meditation

Meditation is simply moments between thoughts. Practicing meditation means to extend those moments. At a workshop I attended—given by a Buddhist monk who grew up with and studied with the Dalai Lama—he mentioned that the west is lacking balance between time with thought, and time without thought. It's during those times with no thought we can connect to one's own inner being and help guide and sometimes soften thoughts. The goal is not to eliminate the thought, just find those emanating from our spirit.

Meditation is the art of looking inside and discovering one's own inner being. Meditation leads us not only to totally new inner experiences, but helps us also to transform our day-to-day life into a better, more meaningful and more fulfilling existence.

Meditation is our attempt to discover our inner self, a place beyond the usual workings of the intellectual mind. When we experience real meditation we become aware of the infinite within and our own unexpected wealth of divine qualities like peace and inner joy. Many people may have had glimpses of meditation unconsciously. For example whilst walking through nature and being awed by its beauty and magnitude. Others may have been moved by sublime music. At such moments our mind becomes still and we feel a sense there is something greater beyond our usual perceptions. As mysteriously as it came, such experiences may leave, giving only a fleeting glimpse of a feeling that is hard to describe. Meditation is an attempt to make such experiences permanent and also deepen and expand our own consciousness.

People may take up meditation for a variety of reasons which could just be curiosity, a desire for more relaxation, peace of mind, or help in sleeping. Others may take to meditation from a feeling of disenchantment with the outer life. If practiced with sincerity and regularity, meditation can give us relaxation and peace of mind but it can also offer more than we ever expected. Through meditation we can expedite our soul's inner journey and we can become more aware of our own spiritual dimension.

Have you ever been "lost" in your work? In other words, have you felt a sense of effortless attention, of total immersion in a task or activity, in which you lose all sense of time? This phenomenon, often called "flow," is a meditation. This is well understood in many traditionally Eastern physical disciplines, such as Tai Chi, which focuses on becoming lost in the grace of your own movement. Martial arts such as Karate and Tae Kwon Do also have meditation in the soul of their teachings.

To begin meditation we need to learn the art of concentration. Here, "concentration" is different from mental visualization. Concentration for meditation means the ability to be aware of only one thing at a time. We need to keep the mind one pointed and focused only on our meditation exercise. If you try sitting still for five minutes and observe your own thoughts, you will realize how difficult this is at first. However, spiritual teachers who have mastered the art of meditation have offered a variety of techniques to help control the mind. If practiced, these can change the inherent tendency of the mind to wander and we can enter silent meditation.

Meditation has significant benefits, these do not materialize in one or two sessions, they are slowly accumulated over time as we deepen our own meditation practice. These benefits will include a more focused and calm mind, greater creativity and better sleep. Meditation requires us to let go of our presence of thought and acquiesce to the reality around it. The real goal of meditation is peace of mind and positive changes to our inner life.

Starting to meditate is simple. Just set yourself up somewhere quiet. Or if you only have a moment between events, then take that moment. It can even be done while waiting in line. Or taking a minute while sitting in your car before going home can help you transition from a chaotic work day to a peaceful home life. Once you begin to see the value and the impact of these fleeting moments, you will likely become inspired to increase your meditation time, and create an environment to deepen the meditations. I find that if I try to force myself to work, I can meditate, even if just for a little while, and then be much more productive. So it is an investment of time that will result in productivity. As you practice meditation, you will be able to do it longer and longer; just as doing more push-ups over time will enable you to do more in one session.

Begin by focusing on your breathing and let your thoughts drift away. If thoughts come, let them arise and pass on their own, without judgment. Next, feel yourself diving deep within, away from the mind. If you like you can visualize a beautiful garden or vast ocean. Then try to hold this awareness with one pointed concentration. If you hear external noise, don't let it distract you; it will always be there. Incorporate the sounds into your meditation. Instead of resisting the environment, welcome it and invite it in. Hear the bustle of people as ocean waves, and bells and chimes as winds through a wind-chime. Hear the chatter of people as birds, or as people in the distance as you sit in your serene spot on the edge of a crowd or street. Then begin to turn your focus on your serene spot and the noises will become more and more distant in your awareness. Concentrate on your breathing. Even if this first experience is not fruitful, keep going—for with each try, you will be able to add to your capacity and gradually learn the art of meditation.

Meditation is a process of inner discovery. Meditation teaches us that we are not just a body. When we meditate on our spiritual heart we become closer to our soul. Through meditation the divine qualities of our soul become a living reality. We learn of our inner self; leading to greater meaning and understanding of life.

Most first-time meditators find it strange to sit in silence, to sit with their innermost thoughts and feelings, to sit and do nothing—the very things that, funnily enough, the mind tends to resist. Your thoughts will quickly start to work against you. Simply allow those thoughts to float away. Promising yourself that the thoughts that you need to have will be there as soon as your awareness returns. I picture them literally floating out of my head and up out of sight. To a beginner, meditation might initially feel a little alien, perhaps even daunting, but that's okay. People have been meditating for around 3,000 years, and many have doubtless experienced the same reticence, trepidation, or wonder that first-time meditators often feel. Remember that even the 10 seconds you might have experienced is more than you would have without the intention. It is like a muscle, and after some practice it will become more natural.

Our entire existence is experienced through our minds, and our perspective on life can dramatically alter once we begin meditating. Being inspired to start meditating is very different from actually doing it, however, and you'll only feel the benefits of meditation by beginning and maintaining a regular practice. In order to get meditation, you need to do meditation. In order to calm your mind, you need to begin by sitting with its untamed nature.

It's inevitable: During meditation, your mind will roam. You may notice other sensations in the body, things happening around you, or just get lost in thought, daydreaming about the past or present, possibly judging yourself or others.

There's nothing wrong with this—thinking is just as natural as breathing. Creatively find ways to either send thoughts away or have them wait. Invent a waiting room for people who appear, or invite them to meditate next to you. Whatever it takes to bring your focus back to your breath, your body, and "no thought."

Step 1:

Find a comfortable cushion or meditation stool and mat to use for the meditation ritual. Find a quiet place to meditate in your home. Your meditation place is a sanctuary for peace and self development and should be treated with the greatest of respect and given its own permanent position somewhere in your home.

Step 2:

Set a timer to countdown so you are not distracted by the time. Five minutes as a minimum then try ten minutes working up to 30 minutes. Also it is helpful to meditate at the same time every day, making it part of your daily routine.

Step 3:

Some sit, some lie down, but ultimately, find a relaxed position in which you feel comfortable and neutral. I don't sit, although that is a common way. The goal is to be in a position where your body won't distract you, and you won't fall asleep. Although falling asleep might have been just what you needed. I use a phone app called "Meditation" to keep me from the sleep state, and lay in a comfortable position. If you're sitting, put your hands in the same position every time you meditate either in your lap with the thumb tips lightly touching each other (this is a meditation mudra) or gently on your knees. If you lie down to meditate, place your feet flat on the ground or have a bolster under your knees. Take a few deep breaths to consciously relax your shoulders and other tense areas. Become taller on the inhale, and relax with good alignment on the exhale. Gently close your eyes. Then create the determination to sit still for the period of the meditation—very still.

Step 4:

Fix your attention on your breath without changing your breath; just notice it. This is the anchor for your meditation. Be aware of every breath you take during the meditation period. Every time you notice yourself distracted by thinking, gently guide your bare attention back to the breath and return to calmly watching the breath. Become a detached witness. When you get distracted, return to the breath again and again without judgment. This is the practice of mindfulness.

Step 5:

Now your attention is anchored on your breath, allow the mind to release and relax into just being. For the duration of the meditation the only thing you are doing is watching the breath whilst simultaneously resting the mind in an open sky-like dimension of complete acceptance and surrender. Give yourself time to settle. When a glass of unfiltered water is left alone the sediment settles and the water becomes naturally clear. Just like that, let your mind settle and clarity will naturally return. It's important to let things be just as they are, especially the breath and notice the openness of just being without effort. This is the practice of effortless being.

Step 6:

As you watch your breath and rest in an open and relaxed way of being, thoughts will come rushing in: sights, sounds and sensations will occur; memories, plans, and other thoughts will flood in. All these things are the display of what's happening in the moment and should be left alone, untouched by any effort to change them, control them, push them away or cling to them; allow everything to move freely within the vast expanse of your relaxed open awareness as you become the transcendent witness. Noticing that your deepest identity is an open boundless witness is training in special insight—discovering and familiarizing you with your enlightened nature.

Step 7:

Let all these things just be, as they are, come back to the breath repeatedly, relax and let go of effort resting in your open awareness.

For the duration of the meditation be as simple and open as possible:

1) Simply sitting.
2) Simply breathing.
3) Simply being.

When you're ready, gently lift your gaze (if your eyes are closed, open them). Take a moment and notice any sounds in the environment. Notice how your body feels right now. Notice your thoughts and emotions. Become aware of your fingertips and toes, then expand your awareness a little at a time, through your arms and legs and into your torso, up your neck and through your face and head. Ending meditation is just as important as beginning it—be as patient now as when you started. When you feel 100% ready, stand up and face life anew.

VISUALIZATION

You often hear the words meditation and visualization used interchangeably, but they're really not the same thing. Meditation and visualization affect the brain and body in completely different ways.

Meditation is restful while visualization is active. There are many different styles of meditation, but the style we focus on for accessing Heart Space is all about giving the body deep rest so it can heal itself from stress. We sit quietly and let a chosen mantra do the work for us, making no effort to control our thoughts, breath, or any other aspect of our experience. We have a theme: Do less, accomplish more.

Visualization, on the other hand, is more active. We guide the breath and mind in a specific direction for a desired result such as a mindset, a feeling, or a body sensation. We use visualization as a tool to prepare our physical, mental, and emotional state for high performance, increased immune function, or better sleep.

Meditation can calm your nervous system whereas visualization can reprogram it. Meditation de-excites the nervous system in a way that gives the body rest, which is even deeper than sleep. This rest helps the body heal itself from many things, including physical ailments, but most commonly from stress.

Alternatively, visualizations can help us reprogram old fight-or-flight stress reactions and help us move into a "stay and play" mindset.

Meditation is beyond consciousness whereas visualization requires you to be alert. By contrast, visualization is more of a waking state practice. We are more fully conscious when it is happening. We guide our thoughts to visualize the best-case scenario, or use our imagination to have a full-five sensory experience of how your next high-demand situation would ideally play out. Just as Olympic athletes use visualization before competitions to improve their outcomes, I recommend you incorporate visualization prior to your big life events: public speaking, business negotiations, first dates, or anytime you want to relax and perform at your best.

According to Sri Chinmoy, famous yogi and teacher:

"No matter which path you follow for meditation, the first and foremost task is to try to make the mind calm and quiet. If the mind is constantly roaming, if it is always a victim of merciless thoughts, then you will make no progress whatsoever. The mind has to be made calm and quiet so that when the light descends from above, you can be fully conscious of it. In your conscious observation and conscious acceptance of light, you will enter into a profound meditation and see the purification, transformation and illumination of your life."

Stepping Into Your Heart Space

This is a meditation exercise that allows you to create your own internal environment. Picture nature, or a serene spot you feel particularly relaxed in. First, relax, then introduce, in your inner mind, the image of a gate. Through this gate, you want to welcome entities, whether from inside or outside of yourself, to communicate with you.

Your heart space is unique to you. It is, in fact, an aspect of you; if a space could be personified. Our subconscious is full of symbology—and your heart space is no different. Every single detail you find in your heart space is significant. Everything from the decor, to the location, even to the nature of your approach; or in other words, how and where you enter the heart space (I.e. if the space is a house, do you enter through the front door, back door, or even a window?). Location is important: is your heart space far away from people or close to them? Is it cold, warm, wet, dry? Record your observations and reflect on them.

Ideally, the heart space is a refuge, a sanctuary; but don't be alarmed if at first it is quite the opposite. Many first time meditators discover unexpected things in their heart space. Often, these unexpected things take the shape of people; real people in our lives, but also people that we may not have even met before. When you choose to enter your heart space, take notes about what you see, hear, and feel. Be open and honest with yourself. As you become more familiar with your heart space, you will be able to draw more and more clarity, insights, and peace from entering it.

At the core of each of us is a great reservoir of peace, wisdom, understanding, and love. But because we live in human bodies and experience the real world as we do, these things are often occluded by the troubles and burdens of life. Because your heart space is at the core of your being, however, you will find that the symbology and issues pertaining thereto are the key blockages preventing you from experiencing the great wealth of life in your soul. So while it may seem confusing or even overwhelming at first, exploring your heart space will ultimately prove to be a productive and profound exercise that you will take with you throughout your life's journey.

Spirit Guides

To many people, spirit guides are entities that we choose or are helpers that are assigned to us before birth. These people or entities are often hanging out in our Heart Space.

To others, spirit guides represent parts of our unconscious minds that symbolically help us to find wholeness. And still, to other people, spirit guides are parts of our higher selves that reveal themselves to us in various shapes and forms.

Our spirit guides are universal forces that are here to help us. A spirit guide can be an angel, animal, mythical creature, ancestor, ancient god or goddess, otherworldly entity, or interdimensional being.

At the most basic level, a spirit guide is a type of energy that is embodied in an array of different forms. Spirit guides are archetypal forces; aspects of life which teach, warn, support, comfort, remind and reveal things that we need to learn about ourselves in order to grow.

They are not physical and are not bound by the natural laws of this world. These beings come in different forms and have different purposes. But their common goal is to help guide us back into alignment with the love of the Universe.

When you cultivate a relationship with your spirit guides, they will give you wise and loving guidance to help you in every area of your life.

As you seriously work with any type of spiritual guides to develop life balance and purpose, these guides get to know that you are serious about your personal growth. This may show up as increased and/or clearer communication. Spirit guide communication is a practice and your ability to listen and receive messages increases with dedication. The most common forms of communication with spirit guides are through your intuitive gifts, meditation periods, dreams and telepathy. Occasionally a 'heads up' shout out is given through an actual appearance. This in-depth work also makes you more aware of Spirit Messengers that show up to add a certain piece of needed information of any kind. They can show up in real life, briefly in a dream, or during meditation.

Have no expectations of whom or what will present itself and have patience. If nothing shows up at first, persist and dedicate your time and effort, you may have to show the guide(s) that you are not here just for entertainment but are willing to accept and trust what comes through and the messages they bring. Remember: have no specific expectations.

Spirit guides are just as varied and diverse as human beings are. It is likely that during your lifetime you will have many different types of guides for many different purposes.

Whether you seek to connect with your guides through meditation, singing, trance, psychoactive journeying, ritual or simple observation, it is comforting to know that help, in many different shapes and forms, is always there for your taking.

6. Limiting Interpersonal Patterns

When we work on ourselves and begin to change, we are finally able to direct our attention and energy to lifting other people's spiritual vibrations. In other words, when someone is drowning, it is preferable they get help from someone who isn't also drowning. When we finally feel like we aren't drowning; like we are our true selves, not without troubles but living truthfully to ourselves, we can begin to offer our assistance to other people. This is the great challenge of self-work: making the most of this life by being a part of the growth and enlightenment of others.

One of the biggest obstacles to enlightenment is the "Drama Triangle." This is a concept that describes a tendency to fall into one of three reciprocating, mutually-created roles that perpetuate interpersonal drama. People under the influence of a drama triangle can lose months, years, or even decades of their lives to its grasp: which is why it's critical to understand.

THE DRAMA TRIANGLE

The Drama Triangle describes three possible positions a person can be in that may lead to problems in relationships. These positions are: the "hero" role, the "villain" role, and the "victim" role. With the aid of the drama triangle an interaction pattern can be presented. It also reveals a specific communication structure. People don't consciously choose to be heroes, villains or victims. They only behave as such in certain situations. In doing so, they invariably twist reality. At the same time, they avoid having to question their relationships and basic beliefs. Thus, the Drama Triangle is a sort of uncomfortable status quo that people will languish in until something whether within themselves or the others involved—inevitably breaks.

There was a significant advance in psychiatry after World War II. Therapists observed that many battle-torn veteran patients who had been in treatment overseas regressed after returning to their families. Researchers searching for an explanation began to explore the effect of family relationships on individuals and found that some home environments were extremely beneficial to patient healing and recovery, and that some were extremely detrimental. Prior to this time, psychiatrists and psychoanalysts focused entirely on the patient's already developed psyche and considered the effect of outside detractors, like relationships, to be insignificant.

In 1966 Murray Bowen, M.D. published Bowen's family systems theory. One of the most critical elements of Bowen's eight part theory was the concept of triangulation in the family. Simply put, when someone finds themself in conflict with another person they will reach out to a third person. The resulting triangle (e.g., three-person exchange) is more comfortable as the tension is shifted around three people instead of just two.

Triangulation is widely recognized as a stabilizing factor in a family, at work, among social groups, etc. We all engage in triangulation because triangles help us cope when we are struggling with another person.

While triangulation is an important stabilizing factor, at times triangulation can be a seriously destabilizing factor. "Bad triangulation" (i.e., pathological triangulation) can cause more turmoil in a relationship, polarizing communications and causing conflict to escalate.

According to Bowen, triangles have at least four possible outcomes, two of which are good and two of which are bad:

- A stable pair can become destabilized by a third person;
- A stable pair can also be destabilized by the removal of the third person (an example would be a child leaving home and no longer available for triangulation);
- an unstable pair can be stabilized by the addition of a third person (an example would be a conflictual marriage becoming more harmonious after the birth of a child); and
- an unstable pair being stabilized by the removal of a third person (an example would be conflict is reduced by the removal of a third person who takes sides).

Recognizing the difference between good triangulation and bad triangulation is critical to avoid repeatedly entering into destabilizing conditions in our relationships.

If you can act and communicate from outside the drama triangle, you don't play a role and thus take a more neutral position. To not take up a role has several advantages. It avoids relationship dramas in the long run and thus contributes to a joyful life. Drama is tackled from two sides: On the one hand you do not invite other people into the drama. On the other hand you don't respond to drama invitations from others. Like this, you set an end to the negative spiral in the drama triangle. Therefore, the alternative behaviour is to not take a position at all, but to recognize the temptations and to resist them.

Victim: "It's too hard, I just can't do it."
Villain: "You are to blame: it's your fault."
Hero: "I know exactly what you need, let me fix it for you."

We don't want to be on the triangle at all; but society honors the hero. The hero is usually in a lot of pain and believes by fixing others they will feel better but it becomes insatiable. It will never be good enough for them and they will increase their efforts to control in order to avoid feeling their own pain.

The Victim

People who occupy the victim role often present themselves as weak and helpless to others. These individuals denigrate their own person, their ability to think and their sense of responsibility. They show a weak self-confidence to the outside.

Victims in the sense of the drama triangle contribute to their own situation. They also make no effort to get out of their position. With their behavior they invite potential heroes in the sense of the drama triangle to take rescue actions. A drama victim unconsciously seeks their suitable drama hero or villain and vice versa. There is a perceived pull between the role-holders, which makes it interesting for both to communicate within the drama triangle.

The Victim role is the central role in the triangle. Victims feel powerless and at the mercy of life's events. It is this sense of powerlessness that make them an anchor for both the Hero and the Villain.

The Hero

People that take the hero position are generally perceived by society as generous and helpful. However, they also tend to unconsciously devalue others in their ability to think for themselves and act responsibly. Their basic and unreflected idea of how to relate to others is to give. Only when they give more than they take do they believe they are connected in a relationship. They do this out of a caring parenting position. Thus, the relationship partners tend to be children!

People act as the hero because it puts them in a supposedly beneficial position. Their basic belief in life is: "I am okay when I can help others." They learned in their childhood that mom or dad acknowledged their offer to help and their childlike care. To be caring, they need to be focused on the deficiencies of their reference person. Thus, all people they are dealing with are deficient in some way and therefore need support.

A person acting as the hero worries about others, help without being asked for help, and do things they don't really want to do.

Heroes look for victims to save and often are quick to jump-in and save the day, even when others are responsible. By fixing and saving others, a hero believes others will appreciate and value them for their good deeds.

The Villain

People who favor the villain position in the drama triangle Transactional Analysis are often perceived as dogmatic, self-assured or strict. They know how to invite others to take a defensive role. It is important for them to feel superior. They know exactly what is right and what is wrong and they strongly think in black and white categories. They often appear like supercritical parents or teachers.

People taking the villain role often devalue others. Villains occupy the position: "I'm all right, the others are not okay." This is similar to the hero's view. "My boss will never become a real leader." "My ex is incapable of communication." "All idiots" - these could be utterances of a human occupying the villain position.

Villains pursue because their behavior justifies them feeling smarter, stronger, and superior. They share the basic conviction "I'm okay, the others are not okay." They reaffirm this belief by making other people their victims. People whose favorite position is the villain need to feel superior to others—which often results in a lot of blame. A villain will blame others for anything that goes wrong, even when there is no way it could be anyone else's fault. The idea of being on an equal footing with others causes them discomfort. In reality, being "not better" is an opportunity for them.

People taking the villain role tend to know the "right thing to do," and make sure to tell others exactly what that is. This stems from an unconscious strive to be hierarchically superior: If the villain can dictate what's best for others, their perceived importance will increase.

Many who find themselves in a Drama Triangle make concerted efforts to escape it, only to end up right back where they started; like a rubber band, they resist the limiting pattern they've become accustomed to—which builds tension—and then their willpower fails and they snap back to the familiarity of the Triangle. This happens because it's not enough just to strive to escape; you must strive to replace the dynamic of the Drama Triangle with a similar yet more constructive one. This is what we call the Empowerment Process.

THE EMPOWERMENT PROCESS:

In Disney's Hercules, our protagonist begins his own journey of growth and self-discovery without knowing what a "true hero" really is. His (and our) initial impression is of the stereotypical cultural cliche—the "hero" we see in the Drama Triangle. But in the course of his story, we see something else entirely. Hercules finds that being a true hero isn't about just defeating some evil enemy, righting a wrong, or achieving a just outcome. He learns that actual heroism is service to another, with no thought or hope of payment. Through this realization, Hercules transcends the Drama Triangle and instead becomes both empowered and one who empowers others.

1. Think of a repeating relationship or life issue, one that has occurred three or more times. Stand in a room where you have some open floor space and complain out loud about this issue or problem for one whole minute. Use lots of gestures and emphasis with your voice and exaggerate your complaint dramatically. (We suggest exaggerating what's wrong first to release the energy bound up in trying to conceal or minimize the complaint. Make sure you allow yourself to complain to the full extent you need to clear the energy.

2. Now, visually pick a place in the room that represents 100% responsibility for you. For example, this could be a square on the floor, or a pillow you step onto. When you are ready, physically take a step into 100% responsibility. All the Empowerment steps are taken from within this area of 100% responsibility. Note: If you find yourself wanting to complain again, step out of your 100% responsibility area and complain loudly some more. When you are ready, step back into 100% responsibility and continue the process.

3. From within 100% responsibility, let your body tell you which direction is the past. Turn and face the past directly. Then complete this sentence out loud four or five times with whatever first comes to your mind:

From my past, this issue reminds me of:

_____

_____

_____

_____

_____

_____

_____

_____

_____

_____

4. Then physically stand in the present in your 100% responsibility area. Complete this sentence four-five times with whatever first comes to your mind: "I keep this issue going by...

_____

_____

_____

_____

_____

_____

_____

_____

_____

"

_____

5. Next, let your body tell you which direction is the future. Let yourself start walking or moving into the future. Keep moving into the future (think of taking your 100% responsibility area with you), as you complete this sentence four-five times out loud with whatever first comes to your mind:

_____

_____

_____

_____

_____

_____

_____

_____

_____

_____

6. I can create what I really want by...

_____

_____

_____

_____

_____

_____

_____

_____

_____

_____

_____

_____

7. Take the item that appeals to you most and explore one measurable action step you can take that will lead you toward what you really want. For example, you may have generated the phrase, "I can love myself more." Great idea, but not measurable. The intention behind this very important step is to give your nervous system a new, conscious experience that you will know you've completed.

_____

_____

_____

_____

_____

_____

_____

_____

_____

So, the important questions are:

a. What:

_____

_____

b. By When:

_____

_____

c. When I get what I want, I will feel:

_____

_____

_____

_____

_____

_____

If you were dying of thirst and found mud, you would eat it for its moisture. This is what a drama triangle is like—a flawed solution to a legitimate need. In that situation, if someone showed up and handed you a glass of clear water, you would immediately switch to drinking that instead, because it was what you truly needed all along.

When you get what you truly want, you will no longer feel pulled back into drama triangles. This is why it's vital to get to the bottom of what you are really searching for. Drama Triangles are fundamentally co-dependent, so by finding satisfaction through empowerment, we won't even feel tempted to return to them.

Empowerment is "to gain power." Find what you truly want, and you will find the power necessary to transcend even the most difficult, complex, and intertwined drama triangle.

7. Projection

WHAT IS PROJECTION?

At the old movie theater I used to frequent, just before the movie would start, the beautiful red draped curtains would be pulled back to reveal a blank white movie screen. Then you would hear the projector start to roll and soon there would be images on the screen. The screen would come to life with the stories, but technically it was unchanged when the lights came back on.

Projection is most often unconscious. Sometimes when we are too close to our story—too involved—we can't see ourselves objectively. Or it may be too painful or intense to look at ourselves. When that happens it is easier to work out our images as an observer—by projecting them onto others. We notice people in our world whom we resonate with, and through them, indirectly face older issues in ourselves. Most of the time, we don't realize that we are working out our own stuff through them. Sometimes we are accurate and see an actual truth in the person we project upon; however, that is unfortunately irrelevant for our own self-work.

Just as with a physical projector and movie screen, the screen is unchanged when the lights come back on. What's significant is the images that are sent across the room. Accepting that they are your images leads to significant growth. And if you are the "screen" in the scenario, you get to decipher whether there was accuracy in the projections placed on you, then look inward and grow.

The example I use over and over when someone starts to tell me how upset they are about something someone said, is the "shirt color" exercise. Here is how it usually plays out: Someone starts telling me how upset they are at a friend or family member because of something they said. "Can you believe that she said that I was lazy?" My response, after fully hearing them out, would be "the problem is that part of you worries that you are lazy." I typically get a blank stare so I continue. "If I were to say that your shirt was yellow, when it is clearly navy blue, you would just know to your core that I was wrong." But if I were to say it was a color more similar, like black, you would probably look at it, maybe turn on a light and look more closely at it to make sure that you knew the color. If I were to call Shaquille

O'Neal short, he would probably laugh, because no part of him worries that it is true.

So when you have a reaction to something someone says, you can ask yourself: "does this feel true? Does any part of me agree with them?" Because that person is projecting their story onto you. The same applies when you are the projector. You can ask yourself: "what part of me worries about that trait?" It may be true or not true, but it is always worth self reflection. Using the example of laziness, you may be lazy, or you may not be giving yourself permission to take some lazy moments of self-care—and are a little angry at the people who do.

Once you identify the act of projection as what it is, you can use it as a tool for self growth. A good exercise to do is to choose three people who are annoying or irritating you at the moment. Then journal a bit on each one. List the qualities that you don't like about them and why. Then when you go back over what you have written, you can ask yourself, what about myself is related? What do I not like? What do I secretly admire about them?

Effectively we are always projecting. Always. So when it starts to gain momentum or it's in your thoughts more and more, it is time to take a look at it. Ask yourself what can I change. You will learn when you address the issue within, it will happen less and less. Sometimes the other person continues for a while, but without your response it becomes less and less interesting for them to use you as their screen and they move on to someone else.

INTROSPECTION RESOLVES PROJECTION

Introspection is the examination or observation of one's own mental and emotional processes. Through introspection, we can gain knowledge about our inner workings. Introspection is sort of like perception, but also unlike perception in that it doesn't involve the five senses. We don't see, hear, smell, touch, or taste to gain deeper insights.

Introspection helps people know themselves by uncovering values deep within and deciding how to use them. It allows you to become an expert on your own emotions. Even when dealing with uncertainty, techniques practiced and applied to ensure that you stay on track to meet personal goals. It may lead to improved relations with others at home and work while enhancing mental health. Some see this as a way of uncovering inner strength and power, allowing better control of processing thoughts.

When we are introspective, we can become aware of things we weren't previously aware of. We might discover thoughts or feelings, or we might form beliefs or judgments based on the information we learn. All of this information can be useful for understanding ourselves and improving our well-being.

Be Curious About Others

While it can be difficult to navigate complicated relationships which may have unmet needs, unsaid truths, or undone work, one of the most effective ways to prevent projecting your own challenges is to remain curious.

People who are curious in social encounters are naturally more interesting and engaging, and they appeal to a wider variety of people. Being curious also protects people from negative social experiences like rejection, leading to better connection with others over time.

When we practice curiosity, we also detach ourselves from others' projections on us. Instead of internalizing and in turn reacting to someone's negative projection on you, what if you remained curious, wondering where that projection was coming from? Why did that person cut me off on the highway? Was she having a bad day? Is she going through a divorce? Maybe she is running late for something critically important to her.

The more personal it gets, the harder it becomes to stay curious, because we tend to assume we thoroughly understand those closest to us; the truth is, however, we almost never do. Choosing to be curious about our loved ones and closest friends actually deepens these relationships— because what is often missing from them is novelty. We lose a sense of "newness" about our significant others, our parents, siblings, and closest friends. Yet people are complicated— there is always more to discover about another person, no matter how long you've known them.

Curiosity Tips:
- Work on listening to people without interrupting
- Pay attention to body language and other types of nonverbal communication
- Try to understand people, even when you don't agree with them
- Ask people questions to learn more about them and their lives
- Imagine yourself in another person's shoes

JOURNALING QUESTIONS: PROJECTION

1. Who are you frustrated by? List your complaints here, and don't hold anything back.

_____

_____

_____

_____

_____

2. What's the primary emotion you feel towards this person?

_____

_____

_____

_____

_____

3. Is there another emotion underneath that as well?

_____

_____

_____

_____

_____

4. When did you first feel this way? Was there a particular moment, or was it a pattern?

_____

_____

_____

_____

_____

5. What belief did this person's behavior violate for you?

_____

_____

_____

_____

_____

6. How is that belief still helpful to you?

_____

_____

_____

_____

_____

7. If this person hadn't acted this way towards you, how would you feel? Describe that feeling and how it affects your body.

_____

_____

_____

_____

_____

8. What is a new belief that would make this feeling real for you?

_____

_____

_____

_____

_____

"MAN IN THE MIRROR" BY MICHAEL JACKSON

I'm starting with the man in the mirror
I'm asking him to change his ways
And no message could have been any clearer
If you want to make the world a better place
Take a look at yourself, and then make a change

8. An Alternate Ending

Clearing our no-longer-useful beliefs can be an incredible catharsis, but there are additional tools that can help us move past the life we already created using those beliefs.

Updating Your Self-Image

As you move forward in your life, you go through numerous inner and outer changes. And with these changes comes inner growth. But sometimes, your image of who you are lags behind. It becomes important, from time to time, to take a look at your self-image and to update it, so it doesn't keep you stuck or drag you back into the past.

Let me make a distinction here between "self-image" and "persona." A persona is a mask we create in order to interact safely with the world, to protect our delicate psyche and appear socially appropriate in whatever circles we travel. A persona is layered on from the outside. Think of all the articles and books you see on how to project the right image for success, how to attract a mate, how to win friends and influence people.

Self-image, on the other hand, comes from within. It's how you see yourself, which, in turn, projects out to the world. It is more authentic than a persona, and it's something that you can work with and cultivate as part of your developing self.

For most of my life, I have struggled with a self-image that I am ugly. I truly felt for years that I am unattractive and unappealing. I have used the word "disgusting" to describe how I feel about my appearance. As a result, I have worked on a persona of appearing attractive. I style my hair, wear flattering clothes, and do my best to look my best. These attempts mask how I feel about myself, but they don't eliminate the feelings. The self-image is feeding the persona. Until I address the source—the self-image—the persona will continue serving it. Once I upgrade my image, the persona will have less power over me. If I were to truly feel beautiful, then I would have less energy spent on my appearance. So, if I lessen the power of the self-image, the persona will have less energy.

Once I change the self-image, I begin to change who I draw in, and what experiences I draw in as well. Holding a belief that I am ugly, I draw in evidence to support that belief. Holding a belief that I am beautiful, I would begin to draw in people who see me as beautiful. It isn't about physical appearance at all. How I came to believe it about myself is where I begin to dismantle the belief. One experience led me down the path, and going back and re-wiring that experience is the key to dissipating that belief.

We respond to our world – the opportunities that show up, the people we interact with – based on how we see ourselves. When you have an old, outmoded image of yourself, you behave and make choices based on who you were in the past, without including all your new growth, accomplishments and depth.

We create an identity and image based, often, on the outer circumstances of our lives. We see ourselves as child, parent, spouse, employee or employer, friend, neighbor, teacher and many other roles. We behave the way people expect us to and assimilate that into our image. When we go through a drastic change, we experience an identity crisis. Retirement, for example, can precipitate a crisis if your identity is wrapped around your job.

Another part of our image is childhood labels. In family dynamics, each person takes on a role. You may be the smart one, the outgoing one, the good one, the nice one, the difficult one, the artistic one, the athlete, the charmer. You may also find a role assigned to you at school.

Although there are many other dimensions to you, you tend to take on these roles to fit into the structure and not upset the apple cart. And as a child, you don't have the understanding and power to choose otherwise. And it may have worked for you as a child. Knowing where you fit in; feeling a sense of belonging. Holding that role served you. It is the moments when the belief about yourself begins to hold you back, you recognize you are outgrowing the identity. That is the moment to make a change. Leaving home can be an opportunity to break out of that mold, but it can stay with you mentally and emotionally unless you choose to let it go. How many of us, well into middle age, revert to teenagers when we visit our parents? Or revert to little sister or big brother when around siblings?

Our self-image becomes a synthesis of all these roles and behaviors, until it becomes as invisible to us as the air we breathe. It's just who we are. But we have choices. Each of us has a range of personality traits from which we can choose. If you don't like your assigned ones, you can make different choices that are more authentic for you.

Begin by consciously observing your current self-image and then deciding which traits you want to keep and enhance, and which traits you want to let go of or replace. Notice also how you've grown and how your image may not have caught up. By acknowledging the change, you make it a part of your image.

Turn your focus to what's good about you. It's all too easy to dwell on what we think is wrong with us, and we get a lot of reward for being humble and self-deprecating. Humility is a good thing when it balances a healthy self-image and self-esteem. Learn to accept yourself, warts and all. Work on the parts you don't care for, accept what you can't change and be forgiving of yourself for things you've done in the past. Remind yourself of your strengths and positive traits, and incorporate those into your new self-image.

Monitor your self-talk. We have people in our early lives who spoke to us negatively. Even when they're long gone, we carry on their legacy by continuing that negative talk in our minds. If you catch yourself putting yourself down, stop, forgive yourself and change the thought. We're all trying our best, and demeaning your efforts doesn't make you any better.

You can also deliberately create a new image for yourself based on where and who you want to be. You can dress a certain way, educate yourself about a new interest, learn to speak the lingo, join associations or clubs and meet people who are doing what you want to do, as well as cultivating personal qualities that you would like to enhance. In a sort of "fake-it-till-you-make-it" way, you begin to convince yourself that that's who you are, and you gain more confidence and comfort in your new role. Then, when the opportunity comes, you're ready.

As you go through this process, there are a couple of things to look out for.

When you achieve something, you have a wave of excitement, a period where you feel greater than you were, and for a time, you ride the wave. But eventually, it subsides. You "absorb" the new achievement, and you settle back to your normal way of feeling about yourself. For example, if you feel you're never good enough, you may achieve something that disproves that, but once the glow wears off, you once again feel not good enough. Your accomplishment was great, but you'll never live up to it or surpass it.

It's important to take the time to acknowledge the new level of growth and achievement, perhaps by marking it with a ritual of some sort, and consciously making it a part of your new self. How does it change the way you feel about yourself? The way you behave? The new challenges you take on? The way you are with other people? Actively acknowledge your success, give yourself credit for it and then update your self-image to include the new skills, accomplishments and inner changes you've achieved.

You also need to be aware that there are people in your life who won't welcome changes in you; they're comfortable with you just the way you are. When we get into a relationship with someone, a certain dynamic takes place between you, like pieces of a puzzle that fit together. When one of us changes, it shifts the dynamic balance, and the other person might not like it. If they're not willing to adjust, the relationship may experience friction or fall apart.

While we can't control how other people see us, we can control how we see ourselves. When you carry a certain self-image, people begin to treat you like you *are* that person, which reinforces it even further. When your self-image is a positive one, it puts you into an upward spiral, and you can build upon it. As you acquire new skills and develop yourself, you'll be able to take on new challenges that were previously out of reach.

Just remember to take your self-image with you on the journey.

You always live up to your self-image.

It creates a ceiling for what you think is possible for you. So if you're not happy with your results, outcomes and situations, check your self-image, and adjust it.

Improving your self-image WILL improve your results—as long as you act, do, are, and show up as that improved version, too. Just writing a fresh story for yourself and then sinking back into your old self won't make much difference.

What Could Have Been?

All of us have regretful experiences. It is part of living a human life. We often process these experiences by visualizing what could have been different—a perfectly normal response. We want to get better and not make the same mistakes again.

We can use this visualization as a manifestation tool. While we can't change the past through manifestation, we can change ourselves in response to the "what ifs" we turn around in our heads. We can change our own energy, and therefore our future.

Now, then follow the timeline of those decisions. Envision the different person you'd be in that timeline; capture the feeling. This will help you choose to live in the vibration that serves you more effectively.

JOURNALING QUESTIONS: ALTERNATE ENDING

Go back to a regretful decision you made. Call to mind the scene. Put yourself back there. Facing who you faced, hear the sounds and conversations again in your mind. What was the weather, the smells of the scene? And call into your memory the moments just before you made the decision and watch the scene play out. Hold the feeling you had when you made that decision. Notice how your body is feeling right now as you replay the moment.

When blame comes up, it often causes us to feel shame. Let those feelings arise so that you can work on clearing them. We want to clear the shame so that we can find the beliefs underneath them. The reasons why we made the regretful decisions we made can be used to forgive ourselves.

"You do the best you can, and when you know better, you do better." -Maya Angelou

Now imagine if you'd responded the way you wanted. Notice how your body feels.

1. Describe the alternate scene.

_____

_____

_____

_____

_____

_____

_____

_____

_____

2. Start at the beginning of the alternate timeline. What happens next after you made the "good" decision?

_____

_____

_____

_____

_____

3. And after that?

_____

_____

_____

_____

_____

_____

4. What happens after that?

_____

_____

_____

_____

_____

_____

5. Continue this exercise until you feel an emotional release. That feeling is what you actually want now; in other words, it is what you wish you believed about yourself.
Capture that feeling here.

_____

_____

_____

_____

6. Envision the different person you'd be in that timeline; capture the feeling of being that person. Feel this vibration and hold it. Allow it to come in deeper and fill your body, until you literally embody it. Allow it to grow out of your body and into the Earth below you. Describe the new you.

_____

_____

_____

_____

_____

_____

_____

_____

_____

_____

7. Picture the new environment you're in. How does it look? How does it smell? How does it sound? Use as many senses and in as much detail as you can capture, list the things you saw/ heard/smelled/felt.

_____

_____

_____

_____

_____

_____

_____

_____

_____

_____

_____

9. What advice would you have given your past self that would have helped you make the "right" decision? Write it out fully, as if in a letter to yourself.

_____

_____

_____

_____

_____

_____

_____

_____

_____

_____

_____

10. Where could you apply the same advice now?

_____

_____

_____

_____

_____

_____

Remember the feeling of being in the alternate vibration. The longer you can hold this vibration, the faster the 3-dimensional world will follow. Be kind to yourself when you notice that you have fallen back into old patterns. That realization can work as a reminder to place yourself back into the new vibration. Persevere and focus on it—repeat the exercise every time you feel it dissipating. Take a moment to journal anything you might need to be reminded of to get yourself back to this moment.

9. Healing

My daughter and I were on a bike ride one day. She was about ten years old. She fell off her bike and skinned her knee. We were near my mothers house a few miles away, so we stopped and got a bandaid. There were no tears or yelling. She got back on her bike and we rode home. The next day, she was trying out some shoes with wheels in them and fell, landing on the same knee. This time it was a different story. She was writhing in pain. I couldn't leave her side to get supplies or band aids. In tears, she asked, "Why does it hurt so much more this time?" I responded with "Because the first wound hasn't healed yet."

As we see how we respond to our daily hurts, we can look at which ones seem to be a little disproportionate. Which ones carry a little more energy? We can look for an original wound that may need healing. Once healed, we can find we can tolerate the daily hurts so much more easily.

Psychological trauma occurs as the result of an extraordinarily stressful event that diminishes or destroys your sense of security and involves a threat to life or safety. Traumatic experiences exceed your ability to cope, and your ability to integrate emotions involved with the experience. Psychological trauma can cause you to feel helpless and leave you struggling with upsetting emotions, memories, and anxiety. It can also leave you feeling numb, disconnected, and unable to trust others. When bad things happen, it can take time to get over the pain and feel safe again.

THE PURPOSE OF PAIN

Pain, like all feelings, is a signal. It draws our attention to something that is damaged, out of place, or misaligned. Without pain, we would not be aware that anything is wrong with us; thus, pain is a gateway to understanding.

When I was in grade school, my friend's 10-year old brother fell and injured his leg. He was obviously in a significant amount of pain, so they took him to a hospital. The medical staff asked him where the pain was, he pointed to his shin bone below his knee. Then the x-ray didn't show any damage, the doctors began to question if anything was truly wrong. But since he was showing all the signs of being in pain, they x-rayed his leg another time at a different angle. Again it showed a perfectly healthy bone. After another period of time, his pain level was still high. The medical staff asked again to point out the location of pain and he showed them the same location on his leg below the knee. Confused, the doctors decided to x-ray the entire leg. That scan showed a break in his femur above the knee. They were able to treat him and his pain was reduced. Now in a calmer state, his parents asked him, "Why didn't you point to where the pain was?" His reply was "Well... I didn't want you touching THAT!"

Pain is uncomfortable because it demands action from us. We instinctively want to soothe our pain and to recover from it—however if we have the option of escaping our pain, rather than dealing with its source, we may find ourselves choosing that instead. Just as someone with a chronic medical condition may find solace in pain medications—leading them to hesitate to pursue the more uncomfortable process of healing the source of the pain—so, too, do we often choose to cope with our emotional pain rather than address it.

When you feel pain, take it on—don't fight or avoid it. It begs for your attention because it requires it. With pain too great to feel all at once, you can do this gradually, like slowly releasing the cap of an overpressurized soda bottle.

A common reaction to pain is coping. When we cope with our pain, we avoid feeling it. This is natural; our spear-wielding ancestors wouldn't have stopped to bandage a tiger bite while the tiger is still chasing them.

As creators, we must understand the process of healing so that we can quickly and powerfully overcome the inevitable blows that life deals us.

The Healing Process

Consider that healing is involuntary. When we are physically hurt, the only thing required of us is to stabilize and clean our wounds. Once that is complete, we simply allow our bodies to return to their natural healed state. In other words, healing doesn't involve any kind of effort on our individual parts.

So what does that look like? For wounds that lie underneath the surface in our non-physical body, the process is intuitively the same as healing a physical wound. We must first allow ourselves to feel the discomfort and pain in that wound in order to locate it.

Then comes "cleaning." This is now a process of feeling the emotions around the trauma and locating their sources. When we go this far, despite our discomfort, we begin to dissipate the energy that is causing the wound to remain unhealed. By processing and eventually understanding our wounds, we drain them of the energy they get from us actively avoiding them. This stops the "bleeding" in our hearts.

This is where using the Alternate Ending exercise from Chapter 8 is very useful. Using Alternate Ending, we can explore the beliefs at the core of our wounds—by going into these beliefs we dissipate their energy.

Recovery from any kind of wound involves the ability to successfully live in the present without being overwhelmed by thoughts and feelings from the past. Recovery does not constitute a complete absence of memories or feelings associated with the traumatic event, but rather involves placing the event behind you and living joyfully, so that the event is no longer in control of your emotions or your life. Recovery is a process that is worked through over time and in intentional stages. In this way, Healing is a process of active acceptance.

The first step in healing is to reach safety. What harmed you in the first place? It is important to confront the source of wounds and to secure ourselves from them first. Then we can begin to address the wounds.

When we approach our wounds, it's important to be thorough in understanding the extent of the damage. Just as with a cut or scrape, the whole wound must be addressed for any part of it to heal.

Even when healed, wounds leave an energetic imprint on us, much like a physical scar. These scars manifest as the patterns we develop as we go through being wounded and healing. Healing energy flows by unclenching. Look at how cancer patients surrender to their fate and begin living their lives—and the cancer goes into remission.

The final stage of healing is cultivation. As we heal, we often discover new aspects of wounds we weren't previously aware of. We must continue to seek correct support for our ongoing healing through the people we attract to our life, as well as continue to cultivate a sense of peace and safety around our wounds—if we fall back into "clenching," or withdrawing from any lingering discomfort around the wounds, they will once again become stuck in an unhealed state. "Strain out" the malformed ways people express their intention - find their intention, which is almost always correct.

CORRECT SUPPORT

My daughter was student council president and an honor student. She'd always been kind-hearted, a steadfast achiever, and smart, always choosing good friends and seeking support when she needed it.

And then, after graduation, she met an unkind and abusive boy who was still in high school. While the relationship was kept hidden from me at first there came moments where little by little I was seeing how bad it was for her. At some point, both her older brother and myself were called in a panic to come rescue her from his violent outbursts. It was so difficult to see her as the helpless and victimized young woman she had become. One time she called me to ask if she could pick up her toothbrush. I offered to leave it outside, because I had to leave and it wasn't an expensive toothbrush. She said, "No, you have to be there". So I felt there was a hidden plea for help. I called together her dad, siblings and grandmother for an impromptu intervention. With only a couple of hours warning, we prepared what we wanted to say, and appealed to her heart. She trusted us when we said that she needed help, and she actually left that moment for a rehab facility. However she only stayed a couple of days before running away. She called me from the road, and I decided to meet her in Chicago, where she was heading.

I had told her that I wouldn't meet her there just to re-establish the status quo. I told her that I would be at my sisters house, and available, but If she was going to call me, she would have to enter a facility that would help her. She instead chose to go to a friends house in the area. After just twelve hours, I got a call from her. With tears in her voice she asked me to pick her up. We made a plan for her to enter a program that was only for the daytime. So I rented an apartment for a month to live with her. It took a day or two to get it arranged and moved in. The day she was supposed to go in, she had stolen money from her grandmothers purse, and bought a round trip bus ticket just to visit the boy. She left telling me she was going to just visit a nearby friend for a day or two. I knew she was making a dangerous choice. I wanted to force her to stay, but I knew it would just result in another running away. Her plan was to return; however, the boy ripped up her return ticket and she ended up staying.

Those next weeks were my lowest. I for the first time understood the word despair. I'd of course used the word before, but never felt the depths of the feeling before. I wasn't getting dressed for days, forcing myself to eat something. Those of you who have been there know exactly what I am talking about. At the same time, I began preparing for a phone call that I both feared and yearned for. The phone call when she was scared enough of him to need to find an exit. This time I was going to be ready.

I worked with my ex-husband to find a place to send her. I found a professional interventionist who helped us all prepare. We again planned to pull on her heart strings, but also felt it might not work a second time. We wrote letters to her begging for her to get help. I also decided to stay in Chicago for the month. My thoughts were that if I were in town in Michigan, I would immediately let her come over. She would feel safe, and then feel the pull to be with him again after some time. And the pattern would repeat. So staying in Chicago allowed me to force a delay in her coming back. She would have to sit in her new situation longer than she wanted. Which was terrifying for me. My imagination would run to the worst case scenario, and yet I knew it would be what she needed to make the choices to distance herself from that dynamic.

I did get that call. After explaining that I was in Chicago and that I would be back in two days, she was surprised. Her request changed from coming home to just a visit for lunch. Later I found out that she was only able to sneak out a quick message and then he returned from the bathroom and that is why her story changed. The lunch was a negotiation. She wanted to make sure I wasn't going to "trick her" and have an intervention. Which of course I was. I did what I had to do. I lied. I was told to "play the game by her rules"

Since I lived in town, where she could easily walk away, I decided to have our "lunch" at my mom's house. She was further away and it would be harder for her to run from the confrontation. My daughter was suspicious. She refused a ride and took a taxi. She didn't want me to know where she was staying.

I met her at the door while everyone hid until the taxi left and she came inside. She instantly knew what was happening and resolved to get through it quickly. She thought I was going to be the same as before. Where we appealed to her heart and asked her to choose to get help. Which we did, but we had a phase two planned.

Once she refused our pleas she thought it was over but we told her that if she didn't what the consequences would be. We each had to say, and mean, that if she didn't choose to get help that we would not answer her phone calls, or texts and that if she came to our doors she would call the police. One at a time we told her as she sat in disbelief. We chose the order of who spoke strategically as each one was harder and harder for her to hear. Each time we would ask her to get help and each time she refused.

The phase three began. Each of us had an action item that would create a consequence for her. Right then at that moment. I told her I would call her school and tell them not to allow her on campus anymore. She refused help so I made the call in front of her. The next person spoke. Actions were taken: From calling a private detective who would follow the boyfriend around and report illegal activity to calling the police on her for stealing (and then selling) video game systems from her siblings. She kept calling our bluff; only to learn that we weren't bluffing. The police were on route to interview us about the theft when she finally caved in. In tears she said ok that she would go but almost as soon as we canceled the police she started to go back on her word. She wanted to see the boyfriend one more time. I assured her that either way she wouldn't see him. She would either be in rehab that day or in jail. I told her that I would not visit her in jail, and that I would not hire her an attorney she collapsed in tears again and decided to go.

Within a half hour she was on a small plane flying to chicago and connecting with a commercial flight. I fully believe that had she not been on her way she would have ran away again as she did make attempts along the way. The interventionist stayed with her until the last step when she entered the wilderness rehab facility. She spent four months there. The first month she was livid at me but slowly she return to herself. She went from that place to a transitional facility for a year still staying a far distance from home.

Today she is in college studying to become a wilderness therapist or a counselor to help people in the state she was in.

HEALING MEDITATION

There are many types of healing meditation; among others, Reiki is one of the most popular. According to practitioners, energy can stagnate in the body where there has been physical injury or even emotional pain. In time, these energy blocks can cause illness.

Energy medicine aims to help the flow of energy and remove blocks in a similar way to acupuncture or acupressure. Energy healing practitioners believe that improving the flow of energy around the body can enable relaxation, relieve pain, speed healing, and reduce other symptoms of illness.

The practitioner will then place their hands lightly on or over specific areas of the client's head, limbs, and torso. They will typically keep their hands in these positions for 3–10 minutes.

If there is a particular injury, such as a burn, the practitioner will hold their hands just above the wound.

Advocates state that while the practitioner holds their hands lightly on or over the body, an energy transfer takes place. During this time, the practitioner may report that their hands feel warm or are tingling. They will hold each hand position until they sense that the energy has stopped flowing.

When the practitioner feels that the heat, or energy, in their hands has gone, they will remove their hands and place them over a different body area.

The practitioner can provide the opportunity, but it is actually the intention of the individual that allows healing energy in. The intention is the powerful step and it can be done with making a choice. It can be challenging to receive the healing because we don't understand how it works, or feel like it is more complicated than it is. If we can trust in the unknown and make that choice, we can allow the body to heal.

To override our resistance we need to actively relax. It may sound like a contradiction, but it can take some work to relax enough to allow it in and there is always another layer you can relax to.

As always it starts with a comfortable environment. Play soft music, set comfortable lighting, whatever feels good and safe for you. For the body to relax the most, I recommend laying on your back with your feet flat on the ground and knees bent, arms at your side. Read through this section fully before starting so that you can let your thoughts go.

Begin with a deep breath.
Turn your attention to your body and scan from head to toe.

Notice where you are clenching. Can you release a little?

Tighten any muscles that won't release, hold for three seconds, and then release.

Shift your position to move any area that's still stuck.
Roll back and forth, then settle in again with another deep breath.

Repeat this a few times if it helps.

Feel the support of the ground below you and allow yourself to relax one more later into that support.

Then take another deep breath and do another body scan.

Do you feel anything still clenching? This time, just move your breath to that area.

Allow any thoughts to float away and keep your attention on your physical body.

Continue with your breath to any heavy areas of your body for a few breaths.

Let your awareness float up a few hundred feet about your body where you will see or sense a soft golden light.

Allow that light to to float down to your crown chakra, allow the light in. Imagine it swirling around cleaning any stuck places and it floats down into your body through your head, then throat, then neck and shoulders.

Have the light continue down to your fingers, ribs, and abdomen.

Continue the light to your hips and down your legs to the toes.

Imagine the light leaving out the balls of your feet and into the ground—bending the light if necessary.

Follow the light with your awareness as it descends through the earth and rock until it reaches the center of the earth.

At the center, you will find a pink glowing energy of mother earth full of unconditional love and support. Allow yourself to surrender into that support one more layer and soak it in.

When you are ready, visualize the pink light rising up like a beam that reaches the balls of your feet. Allow the light to flow and fill in your feet and fill up to your ankles.

Bring the light up your legs and saturate your knees and hips.

The light flows and fills your abdomen and heart. Take a breath while connected to the earth, universe and your body.

Do a body scan and focus on where it feels heavy or the area you want to focus on healing.

With your breath, introduce the opposite of what you are feeling. For example, if it is hot, breathe in coolness. If it is tight, breathe in space and visualize muscle fibers loosening. If it is painful, breathe in healing light. If the nerve endings are inflamed, breathe in soothing anti-inflammatory coolness.

If you were able to shrink down into your body and go inside, what would you do to your body? If there is a tear, imagine the layers healing. If the walls of your tissues are thin, imagine building layers. If the arteries are clogged, shrink the build up. Just keep imagining repairs and fixes.

Then, notice what's going on...

Are you able to visualize it, or do some thoughts arise? Any beliefs that you notice coming up?

Look at each part where you feel stuck energy. What does this body part do?

Does that mean anything to your current life circumstance?

Or ask: what are you here to tell me, or what do I need to know?

Journaling Exercise: Healing

1. Describe an experience or challenge you are ready to release today.

_____

_____

_____

_____

2. What thoughts, feelings or energy have you been holding on to because of this experience or challenge? What thoughts, feelings or energy might you be avoiding by holding on to this experience?

_____

_____

_____

_____

_____

3. How does holding onto the thoughts, feelings or energy negatively impact your daily life? How can you get the desired feelings without this experience? Allow yourself to feel any negative feelings and release them.

_____

_____

_____

_____

_____

4. What thoughts, feelings or energy would you like to feel instead?

_____

_____

_____

_____

5. Write out three affirmations that encourage these positive feelings. Repeat them every morning or as often as you can. Repeat them until you feel the feelings. Use visuals or what works for you to be able to feel them.

_____

_____

_____

_____

6. Is there a lesson in this experience or challenge you've learned?

_____

_____

_____

_____

_____

_____

7. Is there someone you need to forgive? If yes, what do you get from withholding forgiveness? What do you give up by forgiving them? Write write them a letter outside this book explaining how you feel and that you are ready to release the thoughts or feelings.

8. Is there anything you need to forgive yourself for? If yes, write yourself a detailed and intimate letter outside this book. In it, describe your uncomfortable or painful physical or emotional symptoms; use descriptive adjectives. Circle the adjectives. Allow those words to create a symbol or metaphor.

Discover the metaphor. Visualize, talk to it; listen. What is it saying?

Introduce the opposite (of the metaphor). i.e. if it's cold, bring in warmth. If it's dense, breathe in space.

Uncover the limiting belief therein. De-energize the limiting belief. How have they served you? Turn it to the opposite.

Embrace the power statement, create a statement that will assist you in empowering the new you. Use that statement for 2 weeks.

You can do it on your own because you know what you need and can ask for it.

Let the love out so others can feel it.

Life is beautiful.

PART III: YOUR INNER CREATOR

10. The Leadership Essence

Are you ready to step into the essence of a creator? Self-leadership Identity is the first step in moving past victimhood; the second is intention.

Leadership is the ability to influence people in order to get things done. People seek out leaders—for guidance, but also for inspiration. Leaders show us what we, ourselves, can accomplish, while leadership also helps us to focus and organize the efforts of multiple individuals.

Self-leadership is the ability to consciously influence your own thoughts and behavior in order to achieve your personal goals or an organization's objectives. Self-led people make their own decisions and set personal targets. Effective self-leadership skills are typical of entrepreneurs, mentors, coaches, and teachers around the world.

We say a person has self-leadership skills when they possess self-control, dedication, and steadfastness.

You can notice a leader when the group recognizes that something needs to be done, and that person steps forward with an idea or action. There have been a few occasions where I surprised myself by speaking up or filling a need. I didn't want to step into a parent organization president role, but I also was finding myself speaking up for the group's concerns.

Essence vs. Identity

Self-leadership is the ability to direct yourself to achieve goals and objectives, while also helping the company or organization you belong to to be successful. It involves having a good understanding of who you are, where you want to go and what you can accomplish, and having the ability to recognize your emotions and behavior and manage them in a productive and effective in a way that guides you toward success.

While leadership focuses on how one influences others, self-leadership is about observing and managing oneself. Self-leadership is stepping into our own authority. As a level of maturation into adulthood, we project authority onto other people, groups, and institutions. We look to these sources to determine our beliefs and establish moral codes of conduct. We surrender our authority to the group or tribe to know what is best.

With mature adulthood, we stop placing authority in others. We use them as advisors or consultants, but recognize that we become responsible for all our actions and behaviors.

Self-leadership requires qualities like self-awareness, self-honesty, self-knowledge, and self-discipline. (We'll discuss these conditions and others below.)

Many of us try to drive ourselves forward with self-criticism; this is not self-leadership and it isn't effective or sustainable. Leaders who use criticism or judgment to influence other people run out of steam or keep having to increase the criticism until the people they try to lead lose interest in the project.

Thus, successful self-leadership means guiding yourself with compassion, humility, and understanding throughout your daily existence.

One of the greatest personal benefits of self-leadership is that it requires you to stay motivated and to be accountable for your own actions. Having a strong sense of motivation will help you push through challenges when they arise, which can result in you achieving more than you thought you could. Being accountable for your actions requires you to be honest when taking self-inventory and provides you the opportunity to learn and develop new skills.

Motivation is the ability to work for reasons beyond money or status; to pursue goals with energy and persistence. Abraham Maslow, an American psychologist, invested much of his career studying intrinsic motivation.

He found that most people focus on meeting their basic needs like those of the body, security, belonging, and self-esteem. External factors drive all of these basic needs; such as having access to food supplies, the opinions of other people,

Self-actualizing people, in contrast, are internally motivated. They show a commitment to actualizing their potentials, capacities, and talents. Self-actualizing individuals often feel a sense of mission, calling, or destiny.

Internally-driven people are optimistic, even in the face of failure.

Internally-driven people recognize that "failure" is a course correction. I use the metaphor of GPS directions. We don't consider it a failure when it is time to exit a highway. It's simply a new direction. When we are directed to a new highway, we recognize that it brought us to this turning point. We can use that philosophy towards a business that didn't go as expected and is being closed. Only shame and embarrassment is attached to a failed business venture.

Leaders who become comfortable with the judgment of others can keep their focus on the project as opposed to how to look strong or confident. When Lin Manuel Miranda announced his idea of creating an album about the life of Alexander Hamilton, the crowd literally laughed. That album became the most successful musical of its time. Miranda has said that the reaction was confused at first..."rapping founders?" That is crazy. But they would get drawn into the story of Hamilton like he was. Those moments are what defines a leader. Each time I share an idea or start with a new concept, I have that moment where I recognize people are digesting the idea of "rapping founders" and I watch to see if they are drawn into the concept.

"Only through constant self-improvement and self-understanding can an individual ever be truly happy."

-Abraham Maslow

CREATE VISION & MISSION STATEMENTS

Imagine going about each day, full of purpose and conviction. You strongly believe in your values, and you are passionately committed to a mission.

Because you understand the good that your mission does in the world, you love what you do. You're happy to start your day, and you put your heart and soul into your work, because you know it matters.

People can be genuinely inspired when they have a compelling vision and a clear, worthwhile mission; and these can be powerfully expressed in well-crafted mission and vision statements.

Vision statements also define your purpose, but they focus on whatever it is you want to change in the world. How is the world transformed by your presence in it? This is the "what" as opposed to the "how."

Mission statements define your purpose and its primary objectives. They are set in the present tense, and explain how you will bring about your vision. This is the "how" to the previously defined "what."

The Call to Remain

You may have heard of the interesting phenomenon that develops when crabs are gathered into a bucket. The crabs will clamber to get out, but as soon as one manages to get a hold of the rim and hoist itself out, the other crabs will pull it back into the bucket. We humans do this too, albeit metaphorically—often, as you begin to change your vibration for the better, those close to you will be surprisingly unsupportive. And it is often those most dear to us who are the most resistant to our positive change.

This is because you've been at this certain vibration for a while, then as you exit, others will question your motivations and will worry about your safety (since for them, that higher vibration is unknown territory). People often try to hold back those they trust, because trust is naturally a mutual force between people. So someone going to a new vibration may feel alarming, as they will question if their trust will be breached.

When approaching a period of self-growth and vibrational change, seek out people who are already in that vibration. This is why, for example, former addicts make the best addiction counselors. To grow into leadership, seek out leaders whose vibration matches what you want to adopt yourself.

Self Leadership Tools

1. Set goals.

Set daily, monthly and long-term goals tied to your visions and dreams. Give yourself permission Do not be afraid to go for something big--remember, nothing is impossible if you believe you can achieve it. Once you have set your goals, ask yourself daily what you are doing to reach them. If you find yourself stagnant, recognize the need for a break, and take a constructive one.

2. Be a good example for yourself.

Every day, you are setting an example for those around you--whether you realize it or not, positive or negative. Your life is your message, so to be the leader of your life you need to decide what message you want to send. Take a moment to recognize what you have accomplished and be grateful for the work you have done. Use it as motivation to continue.

3. Be fearless.

Too many people coast through life without ever taking the initiative to find greatness within themselves. Instead, teach yourself to be daring, bold and brave. Be willing to fall down, fail and get up again for another round. To lead in your life requires that you do things that make you afraid--because life will unfold in proportion to your courage. Recognize that facing fear may take energy, and work to replenish that energy.

4. Honor others and yourself.

Being the leader of your own life means learning to be humble. Going out ahead of others is only part of leadership; you also have to go with them. Instead of seeking recognition for yourself, show that you stand with them, and that you appreciate them.

Recognize that following you does not mean you are better or wiser, it simply means you were the lead goose in the flock for that moment in time. No different from the other geese in the formation other than you were at the front.

5. Embrace new ideas and opportunities.

Do not shy away from anything new, whether it is an opportunity, an idea, or an experience. Turn every day into an adventure and work to turn all the programs, projects and processes in your life into possibilities. Everything was impossible until the first person did it, so work to always be that first person.

6. Question everything.

Become the person who is constantly asking questions. The more you question, the more you learn, and the more you learn, the more you know. If you were not born with it, develop the drive to increase your knowledge, skills, and understanding. Ask yourself questions to stay focused--simple questions to clarify issues and facts, and complex questions for deeper insights into concepts and beliefs. Curiosity is an important way to become the leader of your own life.

7. Be courageously honest.

When it comes to integrity, honesty and ethics there is no room for compromise. Make sure that what you say and what you do are always in alignment; keep integrity at the heart of your character and you will never lose sight of it. We are all human, and humans are not perfect. But you can always make the effort to choose what is right over what is convenient or personally beneficial.

8. Find goodness and beauty in everything.

It is easy to become overwhelmed by the negativity and ugliness that exist in the world. But if we spend our time seeking out beauty in everything and in everyone, how different life becomes. It's up to us to see, appreciate and share the beauty that surrounds us every day. And you will find when you are finding beauty, even more beauty reveals itself.

9. Embrace positivity.

There will always be something to be negative about. Instead, practice zero tolerance for negativity. The more you reject things that are defeatist, critical, fatalistic and apathetic, the more room you leave in your life for positivity. As leader of your own life, you have the power to either make yourself miserable or happy with the choices you make every day, and you can start immediately by rejecting negativity.

10. Be the change you want to see in the world.

Everything you want begins with you. It starts within. To live in the world of your dreams, you must, in Gandhi's famous words, be the change you want to see. Dream big and start small. Surround yourself with mentors and teachers.

You cannot grow when you think you are the smartest person in the room, if you think there is nothing more to learn. Always be on the lookout for teachers and mentors in any form. The Aerosmith song states, "Live and learn, from fools and from sages." Seek to be continually inspired by something and learning about everything. Encouraging growth and development is as important to leading in your own life as it is with your employees at work.

11. Care for people.

Make sure that compassion and empathy are a central part of who you are, and you will stay connected to your basic humanity. When you do, you will not only become a better leader of your own life but also someone that others choose to lead them.

Heart Space Exercise: Invite Leaders In

With your journal ready, prepare to enter your Heart Space in meditation. You'll find the specific instructions for a Heart Space meditation at the end of Chapter 5. Wait to record your observations until after you have finished the meditation.

When you are there in your heart space, visualize entering the part of it where you feel most comfortable making decisions; where you are most comfortable being in charge. Perhaps it is a garden scene surrounded by trees, or a conference room ready for a meeting, Then, call out for leaders to join you there. Don't be too specific about the type of leaders; simply ask for leadership to come to you. Allow your mind to go blank, allow yourself to be surprised by who shows up. Approach with curiosity and see who comes in.

Be open and allow whomever has shown up to speak. If they are silent, ask in your heart: What are the qualities of leadership you, as individual leaders, have to show me? When you feel that all has been said, allow yourself to once again return to your breathing, and slowly open your eyes.

Who entered in? Write down their names, leaving some space next to each one.

What qualities do those leaders possess that you find essential to leadership? List them next to each name.

What do you admire about these leaders? What makes them role models to you?

The leaders you have encountered in your Heart Space are actually aspects of yourself. Whomever shows up in this space, leader or not, is a reflection of you and your own spiritual energy. Thus, whomever you see when you call out to leaders, whether it be Gandhi, Martin Luther King Jr., or your third grade teacher. It could be a neighbor or someone who you know, or it could be Winston Churchill, Harriet Tubman, Jesus, or Joan of Arc, these individuals or figures are actually reflections of leadership aspects that already live inside you.

Feel free to repeat this exercise whenever you are searching yourself for leadership guidance. It can help to re-orient you to the vibrational pattern of self-leadership.

CREATOR ORIENTATION WORKSHEET

Describe a recent problem you experienced.

_____

_____

_____

_____

_____

Who or what showed up as the villain?

_____

_____

_____

_____

_____

Was there a hero? If so, describe them.

_____

_____

_____

_____

_____

What was your inner state? How did you feel?

_____

_____

_____

_____

_____

What was your behavior?

_____

_____

_____

_____

_____

Did you notice any beliefs you held around this problem?

_____

_____

_____

_____

_____

What was your mind telling you - What was your self-talk?

_____

_____

_____

_____

What do you want? What is your vision?

_____

_____

_____

_____

_____

_____

If you got what you wanted, how would you feel?

_____

_____

_____

_____

_____

_____

_____

_____

_____

_____

_____

_____

What is the first step you will take to getting what you want?

_____

_____

_____

_____

_____

_____

_____

_____

_____

_____

_____

11. Inward Communication

I was on a flight with my daughter—she was around four years old—and she didn't want to wear the seatbelt. I told her that it wasn't my rule, it was the captain's rule. She didn't believe me and continued resisting. The flight attendant saw my struggle and also assured her that the captain wanted her to buckle in. She asked, is he on the flight? Once convinced he was in the cockpit, she buckled in for the whole flight. She even took convincing that it was ok to unbuckle to go to the bathroom.

On the next flight with her weeks later, she started getting nervous. She was repeatedly asking "Do you think the captain is on the flight?" She kept going on and on about the captain.... Where is he? She had taken it too far. Exasperated, I asked her "Do you even know who the captain is?" She said, "Yes! He fights with Peter Pan."

Clearly, there was a communication gap. Her definition of "The captain" was far different from mine. I kept thinking of how terrified she was of Captain Hook being on the airplane. This was an example of a moment where a little more effort in communication could have relieved some of her fears.

What is Communication?

Communication is the process of sending and receiving messages through verbal or nonverbal means, including speech, or oral communication; writing and graphical representations (such as infographics, maps, and charts); and signs, signals, and behavior. More simply, communication is "the creation and exchange of meaning."

Inward communication starts with being truthful and connected to ourselves. Our own emotions are not only critical to our own health, but also to the style and content of our own communication.

Without communication, there isn't connection, and without connection, there can be no cooperation—this goes for cooperation between individuals and with ourselves.

The Purpose of Emotions

The reason we have emotions is they signal us to what's important. They are the "phone ringing" for us to pick up and realize what we need to prioritize. All emotions are variations of two basic, opposing energies: love and fear. Love is easy enough to understand and imagine for most people, but fear needs a lot of clarification. Fear is not bad; it is a signal of danger. Fear, even if it seems irrational to others, is coming from somewhere valid, whether that be a past trauma or a present threat. In any case though, we are meant to face our fears and their sources to determine what is threatening us (even if that threat is from within). Only when we identify the threat can we resolve the source of the fear that plagues us.

An example of an emotion which stems from fear—anger—is a signal that we should protect ourselves and set, communicate, and then sustain boundaries. Anger does serve a purpose. Instead of rejecting it as a lesser emotion, allow it to communicate to you. Anger is a very motivating energy that helps us understand when an already-set (or unspoken) boundary has been violated. It is meant to help us see when we need to defend ourselves. Fear, therefore, is meant to inform our actions (not control them) and allow us to communicate with more grace once the anger has dissipated.

Love, on the other hand, helps us to bond with others. Emotions that come from love include joy, desire, kindness, and compassion. Love informs us when we are safe, cherished, and on the right path. It signals us to serve others and tells us how to do so. As fear is to protect life, love is to create it.

LOOKING INWARD

The first step in communicating with anyone is to know what your own thoughts are telling yourself, and your true reaction to those thoughts. As we learned in Chapter 7 on Projection, we might be hearing and telling things that have nothing to do with the other person. To be able to listen to another we need to have our minds ready for new information.

When we enter a conversation, we usually do so with a certain agenda in mind. With each interaction, we hope for a result. We want to feel a certain way. Perhaps its connection, or feeling heard. It's helpful to know what you want from a conversation. Is it to feel valued, or to be seen? Recently I spoke with a friend about something bothering me, but the topic upset him. I had been nervous about an upcoming medical procedure and wanted some comfort.

Yet my friend had recently lost someone during a medical procedure. Their frustration and trauma was so present for them, that they couldn't hear me. Instead they wanted to vent their frustrations. Once I recognized that my goal was different, I was able to pivot. I was able to set my needs aside, and trust that I could later find healthy ways to bring myself comfort. And I was able to then fully listen to my friend—which brought them comfort. This often happens when both people have come into the conversation with incompatible agendas. You can't listen and speak at the same time. And often once heard, people will be more open to listening. If you can offer a moment of listening, you might feel more heard in the long run.

The four agreements by Don Miguel Ruiz. The first agreement is "Be impeccable with your word" Means to speak your truth. What do you fear if you speak your truth? Remember that the first person who hears your truth is you. Dwell on your truth. Understand your truth. Then speak your truth. This is why in this book we place so much emphasis on journaling—it is a way to speak your truth to yourself.

JOURNALING EXERCISE: COMMUNICATING IN THE HEART SPACE

Step 1:

Find a comfortable cushion or meditation stool and mat to use for the meditation ritual. Find a quiet place to meditate in your home. Your meditation place is a sanctuary for peace and self development and should be treated with the greatest of respect and given its own permanent position somewhere in your home.

Step 2:

Set a timer to countdown so you are not distracted by the time. Five minutes as a minimum then try ten minutes working up to 30 minutes.

Step 3:

Some sit, some lie down, but ultimately, find a relaxed position in which you feel comfortable and neutral. I don't sit, although that is a common way. The goal is to be in a position where your body won't distract you, and you won't fall asleep. Although falling asleep might have been just what you needed. I use a phone app called "Meditation" to keep me from the sleep state, and lay in a comfortable position. If you're sitting, put your hands in the same position every time you meditate either in your lap with the thumb tips lightly touching each other (this is a meditation mantra) or gently on your knees. If you lie down to meditate, place your feet flat on the ground with knees bent or have a bolster under your knees. Take a few deep breaths to consciously relax your shoulders and other tense areas. Become taller on the inhale, and relax with good alignment on the exhale. Gently close your eyes. Then create the determination to sit still for the period of the meditation—very still.

Step 4:

Fix your attention on your breath without changing your breath; just notice it. This is the anchor for your meditation. Be aware of every breath you take during the meditation period. Every time you notice yourself distracted by thinking, gently guide your bare attention back to the breath and return to calmly watching the breath. Become a detached witness. When you get distracted, return to the breath again and again without judgment. This is the practice of mindfulness.

Step 5:

Now your attention is anchored on your breath, allow the mind to release and relax into just being. For the duration of the meditation the only thing you are doing is watching the breath whilst simultaneously resting the mind in an open sky-like dimension of complete acceptance and surrender. Give yourself time to settle. When a glass of unfiltered water is left alone the sediment settles and the water becomes naturally clear. Notice anywhere you are tense or feeling heavy and release just a little bit more, and turn your attention back to your breath. Just like that, let your mind settle and clarity will naturally return. It's important to let things be just as they are, especially the breath and notice the openness of just being without effort. This is the practice of effortless being.

Step 6:

As you watch your breath and rest in an open and relaxed way of being, thoughts will come rushing in: sights, sounds and sensations will occur; memories, plans, and other thoughts will flood in. All these things are the display of what's happening in the moment and should be left alone, untouched by any effort to change them, control them, push them away or cling to them; allow everything to move freely within the vast expanse of your relaxed open awareness as you become the transcendent witness. Noticing that your deepest identity is an open boundless witness is training in special insight—discovering and familiarizing you with your enlightened nature.

Step 7:

Let all these things just be, as they are, come back to the breath repeatedly, relax and let go of effort resting in your open awareness.

For the duration of the meditation be as simple and open as possible:

1) Simply sitting.

2) Simply breathing.

3) Simply being.

Then introduce, in your inner mind, the image of a gate. Through this gate, you want to welcome entities, whether from inside or outside of yourself, to communicate with you.

When you're ready, gently lift your gaze (if your eyes are closed, open them). Take a moment and notice any sounds in the environment. Notice how your body feels right now. Notice your thoughts and emotions. Become aware of your fingertips and toes, then expand your awareness a little at a time, through your arms and legs and into your torso, up your neck and through your face and head. Ending meditation is just as important as beginning it—be as patient now as when you started. When you feel 100% ready, stand up and face life anew.

12. Outward Communication

As a kid, my family used to watch The Dick van Dyke Show. There was one episode my family used to quote whenever someone was upset and was having trouble communicating; in the episode, "my blonde haired brunette," Laura, was upset and when Van Dyke asked her why, she said (with much emotion in her voice), "Well if you don't already know, I'm certainly not going to tell you!" Quoting that line was a light hearted way to point out that communication was breaking down.

When I think about the human design, I remember that anger is supposed to inspire us to communicate that a boundary has been crossed. However, when that anger is let out when you communicate, often all the other person hears is the anger. I use the metaphor that anger is the phone ringing. Once the communication is about to begin, the ringing should stop.

When you find yourself angry, use it to motivate and discover what encroachment into your "space" has occurred. I like to write when I am angry. Then I take the time to dissipate the anger using the tools from Chapter 6. Then I can go back to my journal and discover what needs to be communicated and find a more graceful way.

How Can Communication Serve Us?

Effective communication fosters trust with others. Your ability to listen attentively and embrace different points of view helps others trust that you are making optimal decisions for everyone in the group. As you serve as a role model, this trust will extend to your team and they will feel as though they can trust their teammates to fulfill their duties and responsibilities.

Good communication also improves relationships with friends, family members, and colleagues. Listening carefully and offering quality feedback helps people to feel heard and understood. This, in turn, nurtures mutual respect.

Focus on improving your communication skills. Listen closely to people and show interest in what they have to say. Pay attention to your words as well as to your body language and gestures.

Highly skilled communicators are more successful in life and in their career. They have the ability to motivate others and keep them engaged, convey their message to their target audience and create respectful relationships. Effective communication can boost work performance and result in stronger partnerships in every area of life.

LISTENING

Listening is key to all effective communication. Without the ability to listen effectively, messages are easily misunderstood. As a result, communication breaks down and the sender of the message can easily become frustrated or irritated. True listening seeks to comprehend, not only to acknowledge.

If there is one communication skill you should aim to master, then listening is it.
It starts with your intention.

Active listening and giving feedback don't always come naturally. Daily pressures and demands often overtake our work, leaving limited time and energy to focus on coaching direct reports.

The trick is to be an attentive listener and use your active listening skills to be ready whenever such moments occur. Active listening is a valuable technique that requires the listener to thoroughly absorb, understand, respond, and retain what is being said. To hone your active listening, learn more about our 6 key skills.

1. Pay Attention

Give the speaker your undivided attention, and acknowledge the message. Recognize that non-verbal communication also "speaks" loudly.
- Look at the speaker directly.
- Put aside distracting thoughts.
- Don't mentally prepare a rebuttal!
- Avoid being distracted by environmental factors. For example, side conversations.
- "Listen" to the speaker's body language.

2. Show That You're Listening

Use your own body language and gestures to show that you are engaged.

- Nod occasionally.
- Smile and use other facial expressions.
- Make sure that your posture is open and interested.
- Encourage the speaker to continue with small verbal comments like "yes," and "hm."

3. Provide Feedback

Our personal filters, assumptions, judgments, and beliefs can distort what we hear. As a listener, your role is to understand what is being said. This may require you to reflect on what is being said and to ask questions.

Reflect on what has been said by paraphrasing. "What I'm hearing is... ," and "Sounds like you are saying... ," are great ways to reflect back. The more you do this, the more natural it will become. Use your own words.

Ask questions to clarify certain points. "What do you mean when you say... ." "Is this what you mean?"

It can help to periodically summarize the speaker's comments.

Tip:

If you find yourself responding emotionally to what someone said, say so. And ask for more information: "I may not be understanding you correctly, and I find myself taking what you said personally. What I thought you just said is __. Is that what you meant?"

4. Defer Judgment

Allow the speaker to finish each point before asking questions and work to limit interruptions. Avoid counter-arguments.

5. Respond Appropriately

Active listening is designed to encourage respect and understanding. You are gaining information and perspective. You add nothing by attacking the speaker or otherwise putting her down.

Be candid, open and honest in your response, assert your opinions respectfully, and treat the other person in a way that you think she would want to be treated.

COMMUNICATION BREAKDOWNS

Many problems are caused by how people behave when they disagree with others about high-stakes, emotional issues. The quality of relationships improves significantly when people learn the skills to handle these "core" communications effectively.

Core communications are discussions characterized by high stakes, differing opinions, and strong emotions. Core communications are often typical daily interactions as opposed to planned, high-level meetings. These conversations can have a huge impact on your life. Examples include: ending a relationship, asking a roommate to move out, resolving an issue with an ex-spouse, confronting a coworker about his/her behavior, or giving the boss critical feedback.

We often try to avoid having these conversations because we're afraid we'll make matters worse. And in fact, when we do have these conversations, we usually handle them badly. We behave our worst at the most critical moments. We may withdraw, or become enraged and say things we later regret. But learning how to handle core communications can make you a much better communicator.

We are challenged by these conversations because:

Nature works against us. When under stress, we get an adrenaline surge and blood is diverted from the brain to muscles so that our thinking ability suffers.

We get caught off guard. Core communications often catch us by surprise — we have a knee-jerk reaction and later end up wondering, what was I thinking?

We lack the right skills. We don't know where to start in terms of responding to or initiating a crucial conversation, so we just plunge in.

Our reaction is self-defeating. We act in ways that keep us from getting what we want. We're our own worst enemies. For example, when one partner is neglecting the other, the aggrieved partner may respond with sarcasm and sniping— which causes the offending party to spend even less time with him or her.

But this doesn't have to happen. People can learn skills to handle these conversations effectively. And when they do, their career, health, personal relationships, and their organization or company benefit tremendously.

For these difficult conversations to be constructive, they must have a shared purpose and the conditions must be safe for everyone to contribute. It's important that all parties participate in order to reach the best conclusion or outcome. Many conversations, however, go off the rails as people act out by pushing their views aggressively, withholding their views, or acting from motives that undercut the shared purpose. If you find yourself doing any of these, some introspection prior to the conversations would benefit you. Ask yourself, what changes for you if they agree with you, or disagree with you.

Specifically, there are seven key dialogue principles, including implementation skills you can practice while you learn how to use core communications.

Practicing Core Communication

When you're learning how to use core communication, these dialogue principles should be your guide. They will help you focus on listening and truly hearing what the other person is saying, while being true to yourself and what you intend to communicate.

1. Know Your Heart

In high-risk discussions, stay focused on what you really want (your big-picture goal, such as a stronger relationship), so you don't get sidetracked by conversational tactics such as trying to win, punish the other person, or keep the peace.

Also, refuse the choice of limiting yourself to an either/or alternative (I can stay silent and keep the peace, or I can speak up and ruin my relationship). Look for ways to do both: speak up and have a stronger relationship. Approach yourself with curiosity. Is there a belief held that speaking up ruins relationships. Can you replace that belief with a healthier one like speaking your truth creates strong relationships.

2. Make the Conditions Safe

The first prerequisite for healthy dialogue is safety. You can't have constructive dialogue when people don't feel safe, because they start acting in unproductive ways and stop contributing to the dialogue. To maintain safety in a conversation, you must monitor two elements: what's being discussed and what people are doing in response — both the content and the conditions of the conversation.

To ensure safe conditions for conversation, notice the point when a conversation turns critical, and could go off track due to emotional responses. Look for safety problems (people withdrawing or behaving aggressively) that short-circuit dialogue, and intervene before they get out of hand.

Finally, beware of reverting to your style under stress. In Core communications, you'll revert to tactics you grew up with (debate, withdrawal, manipulation, etc.). You need to be alert to these tendencies in order to counteract them.

3. Make the Content Safe

For people to feel safe in speaking their minds, there are two requirements: 1) a mutual purpose for the conversation (agreement on what we're trying to accomplish); and 2) mutual respect — each participant's views and feelings are respected.

When someone doesn't feel safe in saying something potentially controversial, either they don't trust in a mutual purpose (they're suspicious of ulterior motives), or someone has undermined mutual respect (for instance, by attacking another person, sighing, or eye-rolling). The dialogue can't resume until respect has been restored.

Depending on the subject of the conversations, learning how to have a crucial conversation can be difficult, especially when it comes to creating safety for expressing and controlling your emotions.

4. Observe Your Emotions

Our emotions are generated by "stories" we tell ourselves when someone does or says something. These stories are our interpretations of what we saw and/or heard. Negative interpretations lead to negative feelings and then to unproductive actions.

But we can rethink our stories, or retrace our path from our feelings and actions back to the incident that prompted them: notice your behavior, identify your feelings, analyze the story creating your feelings, and go back to facts (ask yourself, what evidence you have to support your story, and whether the facts might support a different story or conclusion). Also, make sure you're telling yourself the full story, and haven't omitted any facts to justify your reaction.

5. Share Your Stories

Express your views (tell your story), encourage feedback, and be willing to alter your views or story when additional facts warrant it. When caught up in unproductive emotions and actions, retrace them to the facts to test their accuracy.

6. Explore Others' Paths

To have a constructive conversation, you need to encourage, listen to, and understand others' views. Start with an attitude of curiosity and patience.

As you begin to share your views, remember ABC:

Agree: Agree when you share views for the most part, rather than arguing over minor points of disagreement.

Build: Agree where you can, then build. ('I agree with what you just said. In addition, I noticed that...')

Compare: When you differ substantially, compare your two views. ('I think I see things differently. Mind if I explain why?')

MOVE FROM CONVERSATION TO RESULTS

Once everyone contributes his or her information to a crucial conversation, the final step is action. All the conversational effort is moot unless there's an action plan and follow-through to achieve results. This is one of the hardest parts in learning how to have a crucial conversation, since it requires taking action from an emotionally charged dialogue.

Groups often fail to convert the ideas into action and results for two reasons:

They aren't clear on how decisions will be made. They fail to act on the decisions they do make.

To move from ideas to action, first choose the decision-making method:

Command: With command decisions, it's not our job to decide what to do, only how to make it work. Decisions are made with no involvement whatsoever.

Consult: Decision makers invite others to influence them before they make their choice. They consult with experts, a representative population, or even anyone who wants to offer an opinion.

Vote: Voting is appropriate where efficiency is the highest goal, and you're selecting from a number of good options.

Consensus: You talk until everyone agrees to one decision. This method can produce unity and high-quality decisions, or it can be a big waste of time.

Becoming effective at handling high-stakes conversations, or core communications, can make work and your life in general a lot easier.

Important conversations tend to have common signs:

Physical signs - you will display the physical sign of stress and anxiety, for example, sweating, increased heart rate, shallow breathing, stomach ache, dry throat, tension etc.

Emotional signs - you will experience a strong emotional response e.g. fear or anger.

Behavioral signs - you may avoid or engage in unhelpful behaviors, such as, leaving the conversation, becoming quiet, not saying what you really think, raising your voice and so on.

We communicate all the time but the higher the stakes, the more likely we are to miss what's important. In high-stakes conversations you must be mindful of everything involved in the communication, such as thoughts, emotions, words, voices, facial expressions and behaviors.

Also, in these situations the stress response is likely to be triggered and the effects of this can hinder your communication e.g. your voices and facial expressions become harder to control, it's more difficult to structure thoughts, your breathing rate increases etc.

The consequence of failing to communicate effectively in a crucial conversation can be extreme and lots of aspects of your life can be affected, such as, your career, relationships and health.

There are three ways of dealing with difficult conversations:

You can assess how you handle a difficult conversation by reflecting on how you typically manage heated discussions: you may hide how upset or angry you feel and work yourself up internally but not say anything, you may react aggressively towards the others involved or you may speak honestly and respectfully. Assess your goals in the conversation before entering it.

Decide exactly what you're dealing with. Is it an isolated event? A recurring problem? An interpersonal issue? By ascertaining how serious the issue is beforehand you can establish how the conversation will be handled. As an example, you may need to speak to an employee because they arrived an hour late to work one day without explanation but this would be handled differently to someone who has been late every day for the last two weeks.

Understand why you're having the discussion. You need to enter the conversation knowing why you're having it in the first place and what your preferred outcome is. Do you need more information from the person? Do they need to apologize? Does a plan need to be created? You need to understand your reasoning for the conversation because this will keep you focused even when you significantly differ in opinion or experience strong emotions.

Choose the right time and location. A time and location where you can all fully attend to the conversation is needed or the issue won't be dealt with effectively. Ensure that you check with the others that they can attend at that time and place and double-check when you meet. This consent also ensures that you're all committed to the conversation.

Understand that everyone will find the conversation difficult. Recognize that the conversation will be just as difficult, maybe more so, for the others involved so enter it with empathy and compassion. Also, enter assuming that you have something to learn.

Dialogue is meant to fill the "Pool of Shared Meaning". This is where the views, facts, opinions, theories, emotions and experiences shared in the conversation are understood and valued by everyone involved. The greater the shared meaning there is, the better the decision. However, this is not easily achieved because not everyone feels comfortable sharing their opinions and views.

Steps needed to manage Core communications:

1. Approaching a difficult conversation - Start with yourself

When you feel threatened you may abandon what you want to say and instead choose to protect yourself by, for example, staying quiet or punishing others. So encouraging sharing can be difficult - the first thing you can do to ensure dialogue is to work on yourself.

Notice the signs of a critical conversation: First become aware of when you are involved in a crucial conversation.

Return to dialogue: Pay attention to your motives as they may be moving away from dialogue. Ask yourself the following to return to dialogue:

What do I want for myself, for others, for our relationship?

How would I behave if I really wanted this outcome?

See if you're telling yourself that you have to choose between winning and losing, or harmony and honesty.

Clarify what you don't want and add this to what you do want, then ask whether there's a way to accomplish both and bring you back to dialogue:

What you want: "I want Jack to be more reliable. I'm fed-up of being delegated his work at the last minute because he hasn't done it."

What you don't want: "I don't need to have a heated argument which will cause tension between us and won't resolve the situation."

Asking how to accomplish both: "How can I have a honest discussion with Jack about being more reliable and avoiding causing tension and wasting time?"

Check into your beliefs. Do you have a core belief that you can't count on people or are unsupported? Clearing this belief and upgrading to one of "I am supported and I can rely on people" can often change the situation and the difficult conversation might not be required. Sometimes the behavior of the other changes, and sometimes the other person drifts out of your life.

2. Notice when safety is at risk

Look for signs that people are scared because this will consequently ruin the quality of the conversation because they will only be thinking about themselves. When you feel unsafe you will resort to either silence or violence:

Silence is when you selectively share certain information and withhold other information. You want to avoid creating a problem and the others involved in the conversation don't know what you really think thus reducing the flow of meaning into the pool. The three most common forms of silence are:

Masking: when you play down your ideas or you selectively show your thoughts, for example, you may be sarcastic or sugarcoat.

Sarcasm is a sign you are angrier than you have admitted to yourself.

Avoidance consists of changing the topic, not addressing the issue or changing the focus from yourself to others.

Withdrawing is when you leave the conversation.

Violence is compelling others to adopt your views which subsequently forces meaning into the pool. The three most common forms of violence are:

Controlling: when you pressure others to adopt your viewpoint, or you may interrupt others, overemphasize facts and dictate the discussion.

Labeling: consists of putting a label on others or ideas so they can be dismissed e.g. name-calling and generalizing.

Attacking: involves intimidating or ridiculing others.

To personally overcome falling into silence or violence you need to self-monitor by focusing on what you're doing and what effect this is having. From this you can adjust your behavior accordingly. You don't necessarily have to wait for a high-risk conversation to happen to start doing this - start by assessing how you react and behave when you're stressed.

3. Make it safe to share

It's important to make everyone feel comfortable enough to share or you risk diluting your content, or just saying whatever is on your mind without any concern. You need to learn to step away from the content when it feels unsafe to share, make it safe and then go back in.

There are two conditions where safety is at risk:

A lack of mutual purpose and a lack of mutual respect.

Finding a mutual purpose is the main way to make a discussion safe. You all need to be aware that you're working together for a common outcome and that you all care about everyone's interests and values. When purpose is at risk there are arguments, people become defensive, there are accusations, hidden agendas and you keep arriving back to the same topic.

See if mutual purpose is at risk by asking: Do others believe I care about their goals in this discussion? Do they trust my intentions?

Similarly, when there's a lack of respect then a conversation becomes about defending pride and self-esteem. Remember that you don't have to agree with what someone is saying to respect them.

See if mutual respect is at risk by asking: Do others believe I respect them?

Apologizing when you've made a mistake that has negatively affected others. Contrasting to fix a misunderstanding - when others feel disrespected because they have misread your purpose or motive, explain what you don't intend and explain what you do intend.

This is a don't/do statement where you address the concerns that you don't respect others or that you have a malicious purpose. Confirm your respect or clarify your real purpose.

4. Master your stories

The higher the stakes the more difficult it is to control your emotions and strong emotions can lead to silence or violence.

But you can take back control of your emotions by telling a different story and this will lead you to behave more appropriately. So what if you had told yourself that the colleague left because she'd received a phone call about her partner being admitted to hospital and she was so panicked that she left the office without telling anyone? You would have a different reaction.

So if strong emotions are leading you to silence or violence try going over the steps that occur between your thoughts, emotions and behavior and ask the following questions:

- How am I behaving? Maybe you're displaying signs of silence or violence.

- What emotions am I experiencing?

- What story has led me to these emotions?

- Look at the facts and ask what evidence do I have to support this story?

- Separate your interpretations from the actual evidence - it's likely that you've just formed a conclusion of what you think happened rather than what actually happened. Can I physically see or hear what I'm saying is a fact? What did I actually see/hear?

- Re-evaluate your emotions by asking: Is this the correct emotional response to the situation?

Clever stories are what we tell ourselves to justify our behavior. They excuse us from taking responsibility and having to acknowledge our mistakes:

- Victim stories - telling yourself that it's not your fault, that you're innocent and that you haven't contributed to the problem.
- Villain stories - blaming others for everything, judging them as having the worst possible motives and justifying your own behavior.
- Righteous stories - telling yourself that you know more than the other, and that yours is the best way.
- Helpless stories - telling yourself that you are powerless to do anything so you take the option of doing nothing.

You need to turn these stories into useful stories so you experience less disruptive emotions thus leading to beneficial dialogue.

Turn victims into actors by asking - am I playing down my role in this issue while amplifying others' roles? Recognise that in most situations, you have added to the issue in some way - even if it's because you didn't say something earlier.

Turn villains into humans - why would a decent person do this? Swap your judgment with compassion and self-justification with personal responsibility.

Turn helpless into ables - What do I really want for me, for others, for our relationship? How would I behave if I really wanted this outcome?

5. Speak honestly without offending

When you have created the right condition for dialogue you need to speak openly and honestly but not hurt others. It's important to use the GOATE skills - these are especially useful for handling sensitive topics. It does bring the focus to yourself so it can be quite daunting at first.

Give your facts - Start with your facts, as they are the least controversial and persuasive elements of your Path to Action. Don't bring your interpretations into this.

Offer your story - explain what you've concluded based on these facts but look out for any safety risks and deal with them if they arise.

Ask for others' paths - ask for others' facts and stories.

Talk tentatively - When you're sharing your story remember that it's an interpretation and not a fact so don't tell the story as though it's a fact.

Encourage testing - Invite opposing views and challenge your own thinking. If they seem reluctant to share, consider saying: "Let's say I'm mistaken. What if the opposite is true?"

6. Explore others' paths

It can be difficult if the people you're speaking with are experiencing a highly emotional reaction, or if they're not sharing, they're very sensitive, defensive and so on. It's hard to reach a solution in these situations. AMPP are four listening tools that help encourage others feel safe to share:

Ask for their stories - express interest in hearing others' views:

"I'd really like to hear what you think about..."

Mirror to confirm feelings - respectfully acknowledge the emotions they seem to be feeling.

Paraphrase - take what the other person has said and put it into your own words. This confirms that you're listening and you're trying to fully understand because their views are valued.

Prime - if others continue to hold back, mstate what you think the other person is thinking. This should only be used if the other three tools haven't worked.

What if we disagree?

It's now your turn to respond so consider using the ABC method. This tool is particularly helpful when a concern is shared with you:

Agree - find where you agree.

"I agree that these last two weeks have been particularly difficult..."

Build - build on it with something they have missed or didn't know.

"I'm also aware that the whole branch has been hectic in this period..."

Compare - compare the differences between your views but don't suggest others are incorrect - just compare.

"It seems to me that you feel that it's been hectic because of the changes in structure. From my perspective, it's because people aren't comfortable reporting to the new supervisor yet."

7. Turning Core Communications Into Actions

Ideas may not be put into action if people are unsure of how the decision will be made and if people don't follow-up on their promised action. Conclusions and decisions must be clarified. There are four types of decision-making:

- Command - The authority makes the decision without the involvement of others but they explain their reasoning.

- Consult - The authority invites others to provide information to influence them before making a decision. Consultation is important when: many people are affected by the decision, it's easy to gather the information, people care about the decision and there are multiple options.

- Vote - This is where an agreed-upon percentage swings the decision. It's used when there are multiple strong options. It shouldn't be used when people won't support the outcome if it goes the way they oppose - the losers shouldn't really care about the result. Never use voting instead of dialogue.

- Consensus - Everyone honestly agrees with a decision and supports it. This is only used for high-stakes and complex issues. It's important not to pretend that all participants will get their first choice.

To decide which decision-making process to use, ask:

- Who cares? Establish those that want to be involved, it's not worth including those that don't.

- Who has the expertise needed to make the decision?

- Who must agree with the decision? You might need certain authorities to cooperate.

- How many people should be involved? The preference is to involve the fewest number of people that will produce a high-quality decision.

- Transferring decision into action - finishing clearly
- Who? Allocate each responsibility to a person
- What? What exactly is their responsibility - make this very clear.

By when? Set deadlines.

Follow-up: Decide how you will follow-up and the timeline for this.

Document the decisions made and all of the commitments promised.

13. Intention

WHAT IS INTENTION?

Intention is the state of intent, which is the precursor to action. Most of the time, when we accomplish something, whether it be cleaning the bathroom or finishing a dissertation, intent is integral to completing it.

At a fundamental level, your intention is focusing your mind (thought) and taking action to achieve what you want, with heartfelt emotion and appropriate expectations.

Intention is probably one of the most essential parts of healing, abundance, manifestation, personal, and spiritual development. Your intention is a large determinator of any success or failure you experience. Intention is the blueprint of your experiences and the reality you create. The right intention and, more importantly, being aware of the intentions you are setting, is essential, but what is intention?

An intention is a directed impulse of consciousness that contains the "seed" of that which you aim to create. Like real seeds, intentions can't grow if you hold on to them. Only when you release your intentions into the fertile depths of your consciousness can they grow and flourish.

Most of the time our minds are caught up in thoughts, emotions, and memories. Beyond this noisy internal dialogue is a state of pure awareness—this is what we tap into when we meditate. Meditation takes you beyond the ego-mind into the silence and stillness of pure consciousness. This is the ideal state in which to plant your seeds of intention.

Once you're established in a state of restful awareness, release your intentions and desires. The best time to plant your intentions is during the period after meditation, while your awareness remains centered in the quiet field of possibilities. After you set an intention, let it go—simply stop thinking about it. Continue this process for a few minutes after your meditation period each day.

Remember, too, that intention is much more powerful when it comes from a place of contentment than if it arises from a sense of lack or need. Stay centered and let other people's doubts or criticisms roll off of your mind. Your higher self knows that everything is and will be fine, even without knowing the timing or the details of what will happen.

Remember that intention is all about results, not methods. Relinquish your rigid attachment to how you imagine things could play out and live in the wisdom of uncertainty. Attachment is based on fear and insecurity, while detachment is based on the unquestioning belief in the power of your spirit. Intend for everything to work out as it should, then let go and allow opportunities and openings to come your way. Your focused intentions set the infinite organizing power of the universe in motion. Trust that infinite organizing power to orchestrate the complete fulfillment of your desires. Notice any voices in your mind that reveal beliefs that call for things to be difficult or hard. The outcome that you try so hard to force may not be as good for you as the one that comes naturally. You have released your intentions into the fertile ground of pure potentiality, and they will bloom when the season is right.

HEARTFELT EMOTIONS AROUND INTENT

Heartfelt emotion is when you feel the emotion associated with your clear and specific thought profoundly and sincerely. The heartfelt aspect means the emotional energy is coming from the heart chakra or heart space. This is essential as the energies that flow from the heart chakra are about aspiration, reaching out to the divine, forgiveness and love for yourself and others. These energies are potent and carried with the energies of your focused thought. Think about this for a moment and see how heartfelt emotion turbocharges your intention!

Also, it is essential to mention that heartfelt emotion removes the ego. Without heartfelt emotion, your focused thought might be based on ego and non-serving wants, which will not positively deliver your intentions. The ego seeks to control an outcome, which will limit your intention.

INTENTION STATEMENTS

An intention statement is essentially a written expression of your intention. When you write something down, it forces you to reflect on how to express it. Similarly, it gives you the ability to explore what you really mean.

An intention statement can increase accountability, help you understand yourself on a deeper level, and (crucially) reinforce your belief in your own potential.

Good intention statements are typically brief, extremely clear and inspiring. They often make reference to a new way of being rather than just a specific goal. Once written down, they can be used as affirmations (i.e. spoken statements that you repeat to yourself or choose to display in prominent areas).

When writing intentions, try not to get too stressed out about the idea of "getting it right" (as this immediately imbues the activity with a kind of negativity).

Instead, view yourself as playing around with different forms of expression. Plus, give yourself permission to keep trying until an intention statement just feels right. As you work on your intention statement, try to refer to the following seven tips that will help you get the most out of this type of self-development process. As we go through the tips, we'll also look at examples that you can then adjust to suit your own purposes.

Affirm only what you want

Any effective affirmation focuses on what you want, not on the things you want to excise from your life. It's natural that you start thinking of things you don't want when you reflect on the type of life you want to create, but doing so creates an intention statement that includes negatives rather than positives.

For example, consider the common wish for financial freedom. You might be tempted to phrase that as "I will be rid of debt" or "I will no longer worry about money". However, better ways to phrase intentional statements like these include:

"I am financially abundant."
"I have all the money I need."

Similarly, think about intention statements that concern relationships. You'll want to steer clear of statements like "I avoid partners who are bad for me" or "I can move on from my heartbreak". Instead, use statements like:

"I attract partners who treat me well."
"I am joyful in love."

Write as if it's happening already.

If you've already read about the Law of Attraction or done any manifestation work, you'll be familiar with the concept of "living as if". The basic idea here is that if you speak and act as though you already have what you want, it's easier for you to actually attain that thing. Applying this to intention statements, you will benefit from using words like "am", "can" and "feel", avoiding words like "will". Using the future tense makes your goal seem far away, rather than inevitable.

Examples of good intentions that take this tip into consideration include:

"I am confident and strong."
"I am abundant."
"My life is filled with love."

So, each time you try writing an intention, scan your sentence for words that suggest there's still a distance between you and the things you desire. When you find them, take them out and replace them with terms that indicate live engagement with your heart's desires.

Focus on the feeling.
When writing an affirmation, you might end up thinking primarily with your head and forgetting the wisdom of your heart. Instead, you want to make sure that you write something that really captures the feeling of the things you want in your life. Just like statements that use words like "am" and "can", statements that focus on feelings will narrow the gap between you and what you want to achieve. In other words, they will keep you in the mindset required to determinedly create the life you want.

Although simple intention statements typically work very well, consider adding just a couple of adjectives that help you to evoke the relevant feelings. So, a bold statement like "I am successful" can become:

"I am fulfilled, stimulated and successful."
"I am happy and satisfied with my success."

Don't forget that you have the freedom to try multiple iterations until you hit on one that really captures your passion.

Avoid conditional words like "try" and "but."
Another vital tip about word choice is to exclude "try", "but", "might" and "could". These are all hedging words that don't really commit you to

success and inject hesitancy and uncertainty into your intention statement. For example, if you compare "I try to be positive, open and honest" "I am positive, open and honest," you can feel the difference. You are focusing on merely striving or making some kind of effort, not on accomplishing the end goal.

"But" plays a slightly different role here, but perhaps an even more important one. Any time you add it into an intention statement, it negates everything you've said leading up to that point. Consider the affirmation "I spend an hour on exercise, but first I get eight hours of sleep" only really commits you to the latter part (about getting enough sleep), not to the full statement of sleeping well and exercising daily.

Begin with gratitude.

When we talk about "beginning with gratitude" as you write your intention statements, all we mean is that you can create an even more powerful statement by briefly acknowledging something that inspires gratitude. Try to keep it relevant to the intention statement, and both succinct and evocative at the same time. There is strong evidence to support the idea that when you focus your attention on gratitude, the resulting positivity helps you to create the kind of life you want (and helps you to feel better in the process).

For example, to take an intention statement that is designed to address concerns about loneliness, you might have come up with the intention statement:

"I am surrounded by people who like me"
A statement that begins with gratitude could be something like: "I am grateful for the love of my best friends, and I am surrounded by people who like me."

Clear Obstacles.

If there's something about your current intention that feels like a fantasy or like something unreal, look at beliefs you may hold that it isn't possible. Or what would make it more realistic. Or look at beliefs you may hold around people who have what you are wanting to bring into your life. For example, if you want to bring in financial abundance, do you hold beliefs around people who are financially abundant? Are they heartless, or beliefs you hold about people in love... do they lose themselves in a relationship? What would it take to be more possible?

For example:

"I am loving, kind, and financially abundant"
"I am independent and in love"

For most people, affirmations and intention statements become more real over time. If you have a history of putting yourself down or struggling with praise, look at what you give up to get what you want. Can you have both? What would it take for you to embrace the idea of your own amazing potential.

Finally, it's useful to not only think about how to design basic intention statements but also how you can turn your self-talk into productive, proactive intention statements. When we talk about "blurts" (a term originating in the work of Julia Cameron), we're talking about negative things said by your inner critic; things that try to stop you from pursuing change. Often, these negative thoughts are outdated or entirely misleading, and when challenged they may disappear entirely.

The next time you have a thought like "I don't have the talent to succeed", ask yourself how you can rewrite this thought as a positive, motivating intention. It could be "I have the talent to succeed" or "I achieve success through reaching goals.". The former is simply the inverse of what your inner critic said. The latter is more like an argument against what that voice has said. However you approach this, the key is to take negative thinking as an invitation to positive thinking.

ENERGY WORK

The truth is energy work is not flashy. Anything flashy is actually geared at stirring up emotional energy. Energy work is a subtle art. What you see as energy and how to work with energy varies from person to person. However, most of what people imagine as energy work that is flashy is imagination.

Imagination is powerful, but without connection and action, it merely remains imagination.

Effects/Flash (visual or physical) require activating actions, to put some of your energy into motion, so it then can cascade and grow out in effects.

To create light requires a person to set a reaction or process into motion.

If you only imagine without action: nothing happens.

While thinking a thought is an action, the majority of thoughts only trigger reactions within one's mind or body into play. Before a person can complete any energy work, they need first to practice expanding their awareness beyond their mind and body to understand how everything is connected back to them. Over time you will discover connections that can then be tapped into and activated for effects.

For the most part, the only energy people work with is the energy tied directly within their own body. Developing your body energetically is a valid path to explore in energy work. Visualize light around your body and actions to better connect you to the body and actions that ripple outward. However, visualizing light and creating light are two different processes.

Energy work is a real skill, it's like a muscle that needs exercise. The more you do it, the easier it gets. Many variations of energy work exist to explore. However, do understand energy work isn't shooting sparks from your fingers. Rather most energy work consists of processes and actions in how you shape potential around you. Also, quite a bit of energy work is emotional and does impact our objectivity. Try to keep emotional energy work separate from physical energy work.

I am not minimizing imagination; I am directing you instead to avoid getting stuck or limited by it. So understand: imagination is important as the starting spark. But you have to follow through with awareness. You use awareness to protect and strengthen the spark the imagination ignited for your use. Finally, with awareness, you connect the spark to fuel and potential to expand out the spark into something more sustainable.

14. Manifesting

Manifesting is cultivating the experience of what it is that you want to feel — and then living and believing in that experience so that you can allow it to come into form. Manifesting is intention over time. This is the key step.

You can practice manifesting to attract whatever you want, whether that's a successful business, good health, a relationship or even a material object.

Sometimes we manifest things far beyond our wildest dreams. So when manifesting, it's important to stay open to possibilities that are beyond what you think you need. When you align with the loving energy of the Universe, there are no limits to what you can attract.

Manifesting is the process of sustaining a vibration at a high frequency so that you become a vibrational match with the Universe and can co-create your world.

THE LAW OF ATTRACTION

The Law of Attraction explains the otherwise mysterious energetic forces involved in the manifestation process. Simply put, the Law of Attraction says that energies of the same frequency are attracted to each other. Basically, "like attracts like" or "birds of a feather flock together."

The subatomic particles that make up our being are all in a constant state of vibration, as is everything in The Universe. When you are in an elevated emotional state such as happiness, joy, love and freedom, your subatomic particles are vibrating at high speeds. That's where the terms "high vibe" or "low vibe" come from. When you're in a low-vibration emotion such as sadness, anger, resentment and guilt, your energetic makeup vibrates much slower.

As energetic beings, we subconsciously broadcast our vibration all day long. For example: when your boss walks into a room after having an argument with her husband, you can feel her fuming, frustrated energy before she sits down.

Our vibration can be felt by other people, animals, and even the universe itself. It can be measured and mapped as well. In my workshops, we tap into the energy fields around humans and teach people how to manage them for their own health, wealth, and happiness.

The word "manifest" means to turn an idea into a reality. Usually, we want to manifest things that improve our happiness and well-being. People generally talk about manifestation as the process of using thoughts, feelings, and beliefs to bring something into reality, but given the science behind manifestation, it seems important to also include actions as a key part of the manifestation process.

Get clear on what you want to manifest. What do you actually want? More significantly, what do you think you will feel if you get it? What we want to feel is what we actually want. Spend some energy focusing to get clarity on your manifestation goal. Mindful meditation can be a useful tool for this—it quiets the mind and helps increase self-awareness. Or, you could talk to a friend. Sometimes just talking can help you gain the clarity you need to manifest something. Journalling can help gain clarity as well.

Manifest what matters to you. When deciding what to manifest, ask yourself a few reflection questions:

What will this make me feel? Peace? Joy? happy and fulfilled?

Does it feel right for me? (Or is there something or someone influencing me)?

Remember you don't want the thing, you want the feeling that having the thing gives you.

Or is this a step towards what I really want? For example, I could think that I want a college degree, but what I want is credibility. Then ask yourself what would credibility give me? Respect. I can get that within, and what would it feel like? What will it feel like when others show you respect?

Will this do any harm to myself or others? By asking yourself these questions you can choose what to manifest—If you focus on what you don't want, you can do a check on what that will result for you. For example, if you want your boss to go on vacation, or your mother-in-law to get a job so that she is busier, what is the result for you? Does their absence bring you peace? Would it be possible to have peace while near them? Again, examine the feelings you want, not the external circumstances that bring them about.

Visualizing what you desire can help you feel positive emotions related to it more strongly.

And those feelings can help anchor yourself in the feeling more. Just close your eyes, take a few deep breaths, and imagine a scene from your future life as you desire it. Notice any voices in your head that tell you it won't happen, or can't happen and approach these thoughts with curiosity. Are these beliefs that you can easily dissolve or will they take some focus to rewrite?

TAKING ACTION

Do thoughts inspire action? For example, If I visualize a possible relationship, and the thoughts that follow are: "I'm out of shape, changes for a healthier body would show my intention."

Action amplifies intention by putting it into motion. It is like striking a match to ignite a fire. If you do not strike the match, you will not have fire.

Action is also not a one-off event. Action is a process. First, get into the vibration of how you imagine you will feel once that intention is realized. The actions that you are motivated to take will help you sustain the desired feeling. Continuous actions keep sending signals to yourself and the world around you that your intention is strong, and manifestation will occur more rapidly.When you take action, you align yourself with the results you want—your vibration "follows" you. The action taken sends out the signal with more strength that this is how you want to feel. Continuous action intensifies the signal. Continue taking action until your intention is achieved.

If you have not been successful in manifesting what you want, try re-examining your intention. Attuning your intention can bring the results you desire. I may start a healthier diet and activity program with a relationship in mind, but find that once I feel healthier, I recognize I feel better and happier. And that alone might attract more people.

As you manifest with intention, you are consciously breaking through the beliefs which have prevented you from manifesting until this moment. And the changes to the beliefs are what we truly wanted. The desired thing is just the setting, the goal. The stated goal was a relationship, and under that is to be loved. But the real goal was self-love. The healthy lifestyle helped clear the fog and allowed for self-love.

MANIFESTATION AT HIGHER VIBRATIONS

There is a level of awareness available to you that you may be unfamiliar with. It extends upwards and transcends the ordinary level of consciousness that you're most accustomed to.

At this higher plane of existence, which you can access at will, the fulfillment of wishes is not only probable — it's guaranteed.

At this level, your wishes—all of them—can indeed be fulfilled. By using your imagination and practicing the art of assuming the feeling of your wishes being fulfilled, and steadfastly refusing to allow any evidence of the outer world to distract you from your intentions, you will discover that you, by virtue of your spiritual awareness, possess the ability to become the person you truly desire to be.

Manifesting then becomes the business of doing nothing more than bringing into form a new aspect of yourself. You are not creating something from nothing; you are learning to align yourself with an aspect of your being that your senses have not previously known.

When you know your highest self, you are on your way to becoming a co-creator of your entire world, learning to manage the circumstances of your life and participating with assurance in the act of creation. You literally become a manifester.

In addition to clear action steps, your success system should include daily mindset or personal development work.

As you learned earlier, the Law of Attraction is a catalyst for manifestation. It can either speed up or slow down the physical attainment of your goal depending on one thing: You.

Your energy towards your goal will determine how fast it comes to you.

Another way to keep your spirits high is to elicit the support of your intuitive guidance through Heart Space exercises. Through this practice of self-awareness and self-exploration, you can ask your Spirit Guides for the support, clarity, or guidance you need along your journey.

Sometimes it can feel like you've been waiting forever for a certain goal to manifest. Maybe you start to doubt your desires are even possible. It's really easy to give up or change direction when you don't have physical evidence that your efforts are effective. Don't fall into that trap.

It's the same trap that causes millions of people to die without fulfilling their purpose or goals in life. This step requires a great deal of patience, faith, and focus.

If you stay committed and focused on your goals, they will manifest. The more energy you put into something, the faster it will manifest. This can be over time or you can deepen the feeling and consciously send that vibration out with more energy. Per the Law of Attraction, The Universe will always match your energy. If you're filled with doubt, fear, and indecision around your desires, this will show up in your energy and delay their fulfillment.

Know and trust with all your heart and soul that you deserve and are capable of creating the life you daydream about. This level of confidence in your dreams will create a clear channel of communication between you and The Universe. When you do this consistently, The Universe will have no choice but to give you what you want.

I have heard that Jim Carrey had written himself a check dated with a future date on it. He paid himself ten million dollars. Every day he would visualize himself shaking hands with directors, working with them, and accepting awards for his acting. He would visualize this future version of himself until his energy was vibrating as if it is already happening. The date of the check was written years in the future, but when that date arrived, that very month he received ten million dollars for acting in *Dumb and Dumber*.

MANIFESTATION TECHNIQUES

In Napoleon Hill's Think and Grow Rich, he instructs readers to use auto-suggestion to train their subconscious mind into helping (instead of hindering) their goal of acquiring riches. Auto-suggestion is the act of planting a goal into your subconscious mind and watering it through daily affirmations.

To use this technique, you will want to create a clear sentence describing what you intend to manifest. Write the sentence in present and positive tense. Read it out loud every night before bed and every morning upon rising. Say this sentence like you mean it, with feeling and emotion if you can.

This will remind and train your subconscious mind to find mindsets, people, and opportunities aligned with your goal.

You're basically training your subconscious mind to make your stated reality your actual reality.

Your conscious mind can obviously see that you don't currently have your desires but when you repeat affirmations daily, you're telling your subconscious mind what it should focus on creating, and therefore, what it should tell The Universe you want.

Examples of Positive Affirmations:
I am in love with the partner of my dreams and he/she is in love with me too.
I am changing lives and improving the world through my career.
I am debt free and receiving abundantly.
I am a healthy person who eats nutritious food and exercises daily.

Meditation:

Meditation is the act of training your mind to stop thinking. It is a foriegn idea to many of us, so to start we focus on one thing. We focus on our breath. Meditation is a vital part of the manifestation process because it teaches you how to become more mindful of your thoughts so you can eliminate the unhelpful ones standing in your way.

In the Buddhist monk's workshop I attended, as I mentioned earlier, he discussed meditation. He had trained alongside the Dali Lama. He said it wasn't that his culture believed that meditation was better and thinking was bad. It was that we seemed to be out of balance between the two. That we work out our bodies and give it rest, but we don't treat our minds the same way. He believed that if we could rest our minds, they would work for us more easily.

All you need to start is a comfortable seat. To allow yourself into meditation, you begin transitioning your mind to nothing. Focus on your breath. Notice how it feels cool coming in and warm coming out. This helps your mind to stop thinking. That is really what meditation is about. To stop thinking. A true meditation feels like no time has passed at all. No thoughts pass at all.

It doesn't matter what you're focusing on, as long as you're gently bringing your thoughts back to that thing every time they wander away, and they will wander away.

Since the day we were born, you have been constantly bombarded with stimuli begging for your mind's attention. Meditation is meant to undo years of multi-tasking training so that you can become more aware of yourself and your thoughts.

When you grow awareness around your thoughts, you'll be more equipped to catch and correct the ones that do not serve your hopes and dreams.

We often use the term Meditation where we mean something else. Sometimes I say that I'm going to Meditate on something; but that wouldn't be a true meditation, it would be a paradox: because I'd be focusing on the thought of "meditating," while true meditation is the absence of thought. I use the term Visualization for these moments. I believe they are also helpful and valuable. In these we bring in one thing to focus on. Ideally it is more of a feeling than a thing. But we use the feeling that we believe the thing will bring us. For example, I want to believe that I am capable. I may use a memory of a moment when I felt capable and begin seeing the scene play out. I want to focus on that scene until my body actually begins to feel like I am there. Then I can let the image fade and focus on what my body is feeling. Focus could be on your affirmations, a visualization of your goal, your breath, or a candle flame.

Journaling:

If you find that in meditation your doubts, fears, to-do list, drama, guilt, and shame are showing up again and again, it's time to release those thoughts so they don't subconsciously deflect your desires. In meditation allow the thoughts to float away and trust that the important ones will return.

Journaling is a highly effective way to reveal, release, and resolve unhelpful thoughts and emotions. Ask your emotions or unhelpful thoughts what purpose they serve and write the answer in your journal.

Ask them why they are there, who taught you to feel this way, and what they really want to say to you. Allow enough time for honest reflection by creating a quiet space where you can be alone.

You can burn or destroy the page after writing so no one sees your highly personal thoughts. This will bring the unhelpful thoughts to your conscious attention so that you can release them from your energy and refocus on your manifestation goal.

Create a definite plan for the attainment of your desire and take action on that plan immediately. The plan might change along the way, and that's okay too. Manifestation requires you to be completely focused and determined on bringing your dreams to life. The only thing that will stop you from manifesting the life you desire is you. When you are truly ready to manifest your visions into reality, you can use these journaling steps to do so.

Establish a purpose driven goal that's bigger than you.

Create success systems with community support, intentional action steps, and daily mindset work. Allow aligned opportunities to present themselves to you and take action on them.

Follow these steps and watch your goals materialize before your eyes.

15. Using Your Power

With the basics of manifesting out of the way, we can explore the many ways that manifestation can be used to transform both your life and the universe itself. There are many techniques for using this power.

When we think of manifesting our goals, the first thing that comes to our mind is probably what we don't have or wish for the most: lots of money, a body we're comfortable with, a happy relationship, a loving home or family or any other long-anticipated wish or desire. If manifestation were really based on how 'hard' we wished for something, none of us would perceive lack – we are all good at hoping for and dreaming of a better future – but wishing is not the same as manifesting.

Our Attractor Field does not only reflect what we wish for. It reflects everything we hold in mind, heart and spirit about how we feel about ourselves and what we want to manifest in the present. As the energies we attract reflect everything we align our energy to – consciously or unconsciously – we often don't understand why our manifestations are so different from what we are trying to attract. We get frustrated, disappointed and give up.

You are always in a state of creation; all thoughts turn into things eventually. You are creating your reality in every moment of every day. You are creating your future with every single thought: either consciously or subconsciously. You can't take a break from it and decide not to create because creation never stops.

Manifesting requires being consistent. I use a tool from my teacher Julie Hustlar, who's book is listed in the Further Reading section of this book. Imagine you're ordering what you want from a warehouse on Pluto; accept that it may take a little while to arrive. Each time you find yourself with thoughts that you can't have what you want, imagine the order on its way to you and say, "Keep it coming." Use that moment as a reminder to do the steps to feel like it's already here. Clear any new beliefs that may have come up, and imagine yourself with your desired outcome. Then keep in connection with that order until it arrives.

MAGNETISM

As we mentioned in Chapters 3 and 4, energy fields have frequencies, just as radio waves and electrical fields have frequencies. Our thoughts, feelings, and even the beating of our hearts all have measurable patterns which radiate outward. This is why it is beneficial to understand which frequencies are compatible with one another, and which are diametrically resistant to one another.

Like attracts like. If you are feeling excited, enthusiastic, passionate, happy, joyful, appreciative, or abundant, then you are resonating with positive energy. On the other hand, if you are feeling bored, anxious, stressed out, angry, resentful, or sad, you are resonating with negative energy.

The universe, through the Law of Attraction, will respond enthusiastically to either of these vibrations. It doesn't decide which one is better for you, it just responds to whatever energy you are creating, and it gives you more of the same. You get back exactly what you put out there... including the feeling that what you want is almost here.

Energy Tools for Creation

There are several metaphoric tools we can use to exercise our power as creators, but we will focus on two in particular: "The Lighthouse" and the "Love Beam."

The Lighthouse:

In your heart space, build a lighthouse on a prominent point. During your meditation, go up into the lighthouse and place your desired vibration into the lamp. Then, turn it on. Observe your vibration being cast out by the rotating lamp—let its light wash over you, then over the heart space around you. Let it go out as far as the eye can see until it completely fills your awareness and the space inside you. Visualize freely—see the light hitting the grass of your heart space, or the other buildings. Visualize this energy falling onto every part of the heart space. Pay attention to the details to help watch the energy truly land. Doing this daily, you can practice manifesting just about anything.

Creative Power is Already in You

The need for creative expression can be found anywhere because being creative is your nature, no matter what your personality, upbringing, or environment.I always found it both fascinating and inspiring how indigenous women would walk barefoot and sit on the ground to sell their wares, and yet they would conscientiously pile up their fruits or place their crafts in creative, colorful patterns. These women were not thinking in terms of marketing; they had the inner need to create beauty around them.

It is the creative power that originates at the soul level that you use to convey your sense of individuality—your uniqueness—into physical reality, no matter what you are doing. It is such an inherent part of who you are that you probably take it for granted. Yet it is an incredible power waiting to be unleashed for a higher purpose.

The Universe itself is continuously expanding and creating, and so are we all—whether intentionally or by default. If you have tried the meditation techniques we talked about earlier, you might agree that what makes meditation challenging is that the mind creates one thought after another; it is its nature to constantly produce thoughts and desires—this is also your creative potential at work. You cannot stop the stream of thoughts by focusing on them; that would simply fuel more of the same. You can only quiet the mind by focusing on something else— by anchoring your attention on your breathing, a visualization, a mantra, and so on.

Well, just like each thought has the inherent seed of another thought, or a fruit the potentiality for a new fruit or a tree, absolutely everything you think, feel, or do has the same creative potential, and the collection of mental and emotional seeds within your mind shapes your whole life. If it is not going the way you'd like, you either haven't harnessed your own creative power and are creating negatively by default, or your desires and unconscious beliefs are not in sync. You can always change your perception and limiting beliefs. It's a matter of understanding where you are placing your focus and your energy, and what it is that you are allowing into your experience.

Keep in mind, there could be a hidden payoff for how things are now—are you not manifesting what you want yet? It may be that there are benefits to these circumstances. Look for the threads the universe leaves you in your everyday life; there may be parts of your life that are already aligning to the reality you want to manifest.

THE PATIENCE TO CREATE

A masterpiece takes patience and skill. Embracing your creative power to consciously shape your life requires self-discipline, courage, and clarity. Yet what could be more fulfilling than transforming your perception into a life that truly reflects who you are and a planet that supports your truth and sustains life for all?

One common roadblock to developing creativity is the sense that curiosity is an indulgence. Rather than reprimanding yourself, reward yourself when you are curious about something. Give yourself the opportunity to explore new topics.

If ever you encounter obstacles on your journey (and you will, if you're truly working for change), work on fixing them metaphorically. Determine a metaphor that explains the situation, then incorporate a solution into that metaphor.

THE METAPHIX

Many of the most important things in life are abstract: love, hope, friendship, peace. These things are impossible to talk about literally; instead, we must talk about what they're like— we have to compare them with something else. We are always using and creating metaphors to understand ourselves and the world around us. One time describing how I felt in a situation, I explained that I felt like a leaf being tossed around by the wind. I got more peace visualizing the leaf coming to rest on the ground than I did visualizing the actual situation improve. Since what I wanted was peace, I focused on the feeling the resting leaf provided. And a few days later the situation I had been worried about found a peaceful solution. I hadn't been able to imagine it because the situation was connected to so many beliefs that I didn't think it was possible. But the leaf... the leaf was simple and provided a way to access the vibration that I wanted to have. And being at that vibration was what I needed for my outside circumstances to change.

Since then I have used metaphors to access the vibration I wanted to bring into the physical world. When I was moving and overwhelmed with the amount of boxes, I imagined having Snow White's mice and birds clean up my room. Then I was less overwhelmed and in the vibration of "unpacked." With that feeling, I was able to unpack a box. Then another and another and so on. When I slipped back into "overwhelmed," I returned to my visual. If I couldn't get there on my own, I would actually watch Snow White, or another show that put me into that vibration. Or I would go for a walk and see the beauty around me. Whatever it would take to get me to feel grounded, unpacked, and organized. And then I returned to the work once back in that vibration. And the work would be smoother, easier, and I would even get creative ideas about how to organize as I unpacked.

"If our thinking is true, then the metaphors by which we think must be good metaphors."

- CS Lewis

Metaphors can also reveal what blocks are in your way. I imagined a long lost unrequited love coming to my door with flowers to profess his love and I discovered a significant amount of anger had to be released before anyone would want to darken my doorstep. Once released, I was more approachable, and doors that I didn't even know were there began to open with more possibilities.

Next time you want to achieve something, find a metaphor that will help you communicate it brilliantly. Think about how you want to feel and use your imagination to feel how it would be to have that quality for yourself.

For example, if you want to feel calm and grounded like a big tree, you can imagine how it would feel to have the qualities of the tree you admire. How it is still and can move with the breeze when needed, how it is rooted and has the strength to stand tall, how it has the calm presence and confidence of its place in the world.

Have fun with your metaphors and build images to enhance the things you love in your life as well the things you want to achieve. The more you step into the qualities of the metaphors and experience them for yourself, the greater you'll feel.

"Metaphors have a way of holding the most truth in the least space."

-Orson Scott Card

Start with your body. If you tune into your body and feel tightness, imagine the muscles loosening. If it feels hot, imagine cool water splashing on it. If it is a lump, imagine it dissolving. Then notice how it feels to have the change. That is the vibration you want to hold to have the outside world match how you feel. It doesn't start with changing the outside, it starts with changing the inside.

And that is more easily found in a metaphor.

Conclusion

The most powerful tool is the realization that what happens inside of us creates what happens outside of us. The tendency to try to make things change outside of us is a distraction from what is going on inside. And it doesn't even work–it just makes us hungry for more.

If we are motivated to make a change in someone or something in our world, we must pay attention to our thoughts. Notice how the thoughts you have in your mind result in physical changes in your body. The feelings may be uncomfortable, and you may need to seek help from trusted sources. But when you have gotten through them, learn from those moments. If you had a magic wand, what outside of you would you change? And once the change was made, what would be different for you?

We find ourselves in an unprecedented time, but the feelings people had during other trying times were similar.

Whether right or left, wartime or peace, feast or famine, healthy or sick, there is one thing that is consistent: people are people. When we feel good, we are helpful and generous. When we feel bad, we lash out and yell. And sometimes we oscillate between the two daily or even hourly. Even a pill or vaccine would frighten suspicious people—just as the lack of one frightens others. So, the question is: Is there a way out? A solution that we all agreed on?

The answer is yes, and it isn't a new idea. It isn't a complicated idea either. But unfortunately it isn't an easy idea. We have to see our opposition as human beings with valid concerns.

I once attended a workshop for business leaders and it was all about negotiating. The instructor said that the first rule of negotiating is to find out what the other person wants and give it to them. My internal dialogue flipped out and then went into hyper-speed. Giving in was the last thing I wanted to do. But he convinced me that I wasn't giving in, but digging under.

He said, "If you could find a way to give them what they wanted without losing what you wanted, a deal could be made."

I've seen people screaming and demanding what they want for all kinds of political causes. But what they really want is financial security and protection of their rights and freedoms. And underneath that what they really want is support and safety in a swirl of unknowns. Sometimes just being heard and understood goes really far in creating safety. The people arguing with the protesters want protection and safety as well.

Looking back to an era full of protests, I looked at the Civil Rights movement. During that era, it was also a time full of unsafe circumstances and unknown futures. A leader during that time understood the pain of the protesters. He also understood that hate was not going to solve anything.

Inscribed on the Martin Luther King Memorial Wall is a quote about how to get out of darkness:

"Darkness cannot drive out darkness. Only light can do that. Hate cannot drive out hate, only love can do that."

-Rev. Dr. Martin Luther King, Jr.

When you see someone yelling at a protest, recognize that they feel oppressed. They feel trapped and powerless. And they feel unsafe. If you can see that–if you can feel compassion for them–then that is better than adding inflammatory comments to the mix. Recognize that for someone to change their beliefs is an incredible shift.

And then ask yourself, what would change for you if they did change their beliefs? How is your life better if someone else changes their mind? What if they actually put down their signs and agreed with you? How does your life truly change? If you can answer that question, then you can find what you really want deep down.

My guess is it is some form of peace, love, freedom, or joy. Whatever it is, find a way to connect to that feeling on your own. Take your power back from external sources, and give yourself that peace or joy. Find the feeling of freedom and love with your intention alone.

Desire is a guide to let you know how you want to feel. Once you know that, you can open up to the possibilities. There are so many ways to get that feeling.

When you capture that feeling, it will be contagious and magnetic and your external world will start to match the internal world.

The changes might not be what you expected or how you envisioned them; but they will support your new way of being, and will influence those around you. Sometimes PEOPLE change and sometimes people CHANGE.

You will not only be feeling the peace, love and joy—you will be sharing it.

Further Reading

The Mask, the Mirror, and the Illusion - Julie Hutslar
A wonderful entry into this work. This book contains many of the tools mentioned and more. It is a practical and relatable guide to getting in touch with your spirit.

The Four Agreements - Don Miguel Ruiz
A simple way to change your life is to read this book. These agreements should be taught in kindergarten.

Loving What Is - Byron Katie
When you don't like what's going on in your life, this book can help shift your perspective from negative and discouraged to positive and appreciative.

Anatomy of the Spirit - Caroline Myss
This book connects you to your body and spirit. It relates your spirit and emotions to physical symptoms and diseases.

Heal Your Body - Louise Hay
A reference book that helps you see what is behind physical symptoms and allows you to either heal or help heal yourself from the source. I use it in conjunction with western meds to come at healing from both angles.

A Brief History of Everything - Ken Wilber
An overview of human development that shows where you are and allows you to accept others where they are. A difficult read, but packed with so much information about how humans think, feel and relate to each other.

A Whole New Mind - Daniel Pink
Coming from a left-brained engineer's mind, this book opened me up to embrace and appreciate the creative side of our brains and to allow both sides to work in harmony.

On Becoming a Person: A Therapist's View of Psychotherapy - Carl Rogers
A must read if you want to be a coach, and a great book if you want to be a better friend.

In a Different Voice: Psychological Theory and Women's Development - Carol Gilligan
Opened my eyes to how women's minds work, and allowed me to accept the way my own mind works.

Urgent Message from Mother - Jean Shinoda Bolen
This book inspires you to embrace yourself as you are, and to gather with others to help improve both your world and our world.

Dignity - Donna Hicks
From someone who avoided conflict, it inspires me to find a way to honor everyone involved so that we all benefit from facing them.

Modern Man In Search of a Soul - Carl Jung
An insightful look into what is truly important in the human experience.

The War of Art - Stephen Pressfield
If you have that project that you just can't finish, this book will help you over the goal line. Any creation we make has to be introduced into the world. This book helps you overcome whatever is holding you back.

Gratitude

My Friends & Family:

My parents - each day, I appreciate you more and more. The more people I meet the more I recognize how amazing you were from childhood on. I miss you both.

Laurie E - Always ready with a way through when I feel overwhelmed. Kept me grounded and connected with family. The best listener on the weekly sibling zoom.

Julie G - Ready with "You got this" when I had metaphorical labor contractions (& the real ones). The strongest encouragement on the weekly sibling zoom.

Rick B - The quickest wit on the weekly sibling zoom.

Pam B - The biggest heart on the weekly sibling zoom.

Fred & Mary; Mira & Shannon - my second family. Grateful to you all for welcoming me into your family and deepening the family history.

Barbara M - That rare lifelong confidant. You have been there for me through all the ups and downs... and listened to all the stories as they unfold.

Karen V - Ever supportive... even the crazy ideas. Especially the ideas that I feel profoundly.

Kathy R - Such a safe listener and so amazing in a crisis... like in a broken down car in Guatemala with a baby and a toddler.

Shirlee H - You trusted me enough to allow me to practice with each new training.

Roger C - Opened up my mind to a world view and brought the kids into that expanded view.

Dauray O - When you handed me the book Urgent Message from Mother, you changed my life. It was the first step towards honoring my feminine side.

Cynthia Goerig Stamation - You help me discover who I truly am. Over and over.

Rorie L - My community and companion when I felt the most alone.

Mickie T - You showed me how to celebrate with exuberant joy.

Heather R - You remind me that ambition and femininity can combine and be fun.

Earlene & David - You show me how to build a community based on love and acceptance.

Becky L - You help me draw down to the root of what I want my impact to be on the world.

Meg, Emily, and Pamela - You helped me offer the precious gift of starting an introspective journey towards self love to many many women.

All the Mariposa Ladies - You inspire me to face my fears with the courage and grace that you face yours.

Jen Mac - You show me that being visible can be fun. I still want to be you when I am on stage.

Bree W - You appreciate my philosophy and coaching so much that it inspired me to share it and write this book.

Alex R - You rode this ride with me, experiencing each chapter as it was written.

Jim K - The kindest guy I know. You inspire me to be a more authentic version of myself.

My kids: Eric, Rebeca, & Evie - You are each amazing and inspiring adults. You taught me how to love unconditionally. That I did have it in me to fight the fights to keep you safe and healthy. And that the fights are worth it and even appreciated. Eric you are so thoughtful and protective; Rebeca you are so connecting and caring; Evie you are so brave and self-aware. Love you beyond words.